STUDIES IN THE GERMANIC LANGUAGES AND LITERATURES

Number 2

THE EARLY GERMAN EPIGRAM

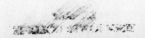

THE EARLY GERMAN EPIGRAM

A STUDY IN BAROQUE POETRY

BY

R. K. ANGRESS

THE UNIVERSITY PRESS OF KENTUCKY

LEXINGTON, 1971

Standard Book Number 8131-1231-1
Library of Congress Catalog Card Number 70-111501

A statewide cooperative scholarly publishing agency serving Berea College, Centre College of Kentucky, Eastern Kentucky University, Kentucky State College, Morehead State University, Murray State University, University of Kentucky, University of Louisville, and Western Kentucky University

Editorial and Sales Offices: Lexington, Kentucky 40506

PRINTED IN SPAIN

DEPÓSITO LEGAL: V. 4.037 - 1971

Artes Gráficas Soler, S. A. — Jávea, 28 — Valencia (8) — 1971

To Liselotte Marshall and Monique Weil
in lasting friendship

CONTENTS

ACKNOWLEDGMENTS

It was my good fortune to write this study with the help and encouragement of a number of scholars and friends. Foremost among these is Professor Blake Lee Spahr of the University of California whose patient and knowledgeable criticism has left an impression on every chapter of this book. I further wish to thank Professor Ehrhard Bahr of the University of California at Los Angeles for many fruitful discussions that helped give shape to it; Mrs. Roselinde Konrad of the University of California at Santa Barbara, who helped in proofreading the manuscript and on whose patience and friendship I greatly depended while writing the last chapters; and Professor Marvin Schindler of the University of Virginia, whose close reading and informed comments were of invaluable help in the final revision.

Acknowledgment is due to New Directions Publishing Corporation for permission to quote "Epitaph of a young child" from *Poems from the Greek Anthology* by Dudley Fitts; to Penguin Books Limited for two poems from the *Penguin Book of Japanese Verse;* and to Suhrkamp Verlag for Bertolt Brecht's "Der Rauch" and "Die Maske des Bösen" from Brecht, *Gedichte und Lieder.*

INTRODUCTION

NO COMPREHENSIVE STUDY OF THE SEVENTEENTH-CENTURY GERMAN EPIGRAM EXISTS, although scholars have for more than a century been in perfect accordance as to the importance of the subject. In 1842 G. G. Gervinus wrote: "Epigramm und Kirchenlied bilden im Grunde die Spitzen der ganzen schlesischen Poesie." [1] Eighty years later, at the beginning of modern Baroque scholarship, Herbert Cysarz stated succinctly: "Das Epigramm bleibt eine Urform des Barock." [2] More recently Wolfgang Preisendanz has repeated this view, claiming that from the time of Opitz onward, the epigram became "eine bevorzugte und stellenweise dominierende Form der Lyrik." [3]

In spite of this agreement, the seventeenth-century epigram has been treated only in a haphazard, incidental, or fragmentary fashion. The reason for this may well be the pervasive influence of two books that have long outlived their usefulness, Max Waldberg's *Die galante Lyrik* [4] and its successor, *Die deutsche Renaissance-Lyrik*. To Waldberg Baroque poetry was a morass "in dessen giftigen Dünsten für die Epigonen des Dreissigjährigen Krieges die 'Blümchen nach italienischer Art' üppig gedeihen." [5] The epigram in

---

[1] He added with frank partiality: "und zugleich ihre erfreulichste Seite." Georg Gottfried Gervinus, *Handbuch der Geschichte der poetischen National-Literatur der Deutschen* (Leipzig, 1842), p. 153.

[2] Herbert Cysarz, *Deutsche Barockdichtung* (Leipzig, 1924), p. 9.

[3] Wolfgang Preisendanz, *Die Spruchform in der Lyrik des alten Goethe und ihre Vorgeschichte seit Opitz* (Heidelberg, 1952), p. 29 (hereafter cited as *Spruchform*).

[4] Max Waldberg, *Die galante Lyrik*, Quellen und Forschungen zur Sprach- und Culturgeschichte der germanischen Völker, vol. 56 (Strasburg, 1885).

[5] Max Waldberg, *Die deutsche Renaissance-Lyrik* (Berlin, 1888), p. 82 (hereafter cited as *Renaissance-Lyrik*).

particular was a bottomless pit of unscrupulous plagiarism.[6] Waldberg set the tone for a number of studies that are notable for their hostility toward the subject they treat.

At the turn of the century three such studies of the epigram appeared. All three deal with related aspects of one theme: the derivation of German epigrams from classical and Neo-Latin authors. All three are admirable for their painstaking work and thoroughness, but all of them are marred by their dislike of the baroque age and style. Erich Urban, in his *Owenus und die deutschen Epigrammatiker des XVII. Jahrhunderts,* was the worst offender. He showed convincingly and in some detail that the influence of the Neo-Latin Scottish poet John Owen was probably even greater than that of Martial. Then he summed up his contempt for the epigram as follows: "Man berauschte sich lange daran, das ganze XVII. Jahrhundert hindurch und noch länger, bis eine neue Zeit anbrach, die dem Kleinkram der Poesie den Platz anwies, der ihm gebührte." By his own statement, Urban's contribution was to be explicitly negative. He aimed to show "den unheilvollen Einfluss, den Owenus auf die deutschen Epigrammatiker übt."[7] He was curiously blind to such matters as the variety of verse forms and the general joy in form experiments typical of the German epigrammatists of this time. So he wrote: "Der Vers des deutschen Epigrammatikers erregt daher kein tieferes Interesse: er ist gleichförmig, nach der Schablone gemacht und ohne persönliche Momente. Nur ungern geht man von dem beliebtesten Maße, dem Alexandriner ab."[8]

Very similar, though less vehement, is Richard Levy's careful but inconclusive Heidelberg dissertation, *Martial und die deutsche Epigrammatik des siebzehnten Jahrhunderts* (Stuttgart, 1903). The third book in this group is Max Rubensohn's *Griechische Epigramme und andere kleinere Dichtungen in deutschen Übersetzungen des XVI. und XVII. Jahrhunderts.*[9] Similar studies can be found for

---

[6] Waldberg, *Galante Lyrik,* pp. 120-21; Waldberg, *Renaissance-Lyrik,* pp. 210-14.

[7] Erich Urban, *Owenus und die deutsche Epigrammatiker des XVII. Jahrhunderts,* Litterarhistorische Forschungen, vol. II (Berlin, 1900), pp. 6, 33 (hereafter cited as *Owenus*). Waldberg was co-editor of this series, a fact which may partly account for the tone.

[8] Waldberg, *Renaissance-Lyrik,* p. 34.

[9] In Bibliothek älterer deutscher Übersetzungen, vols. 2-5 (Weimar, 1897).

specific poets. [10] But useful and informative as these are, they have contributed to the unfavorable reputation of the seventeenth-century epigram by stressing, and often censuring, its least interesting aspect.

These studies are highly specialized and will not help the reader to find his way through the confusing mass of material that confronts him or to form an opinion on the merits and significance of the genre. Some general critical guidelines are sorely needed, but they are not to be found where one would expect to find them. Axel Lindqvist's *Det tyske 1600-Talsepigrammets motiv och tendenser några Konturer,* the only book which promises in its title to cover the subject, is disappointing. [11] The author, who is also the editor of the epigrams of Johann Grob, deals in well-worn generalizations of a sociological kind and concentrates on Logau, Grob, and Wernicke. Moreover, he leans heavily on the findings of Urban and Levy. Erik Lunding sharply criticized this book, when it first appeared, as being out of touch with modern Baroque scholarship. [12]

On the other hand, Wolfgang Preisendanz's book, which ordinarily does not even appear in Baroque bibliographies because it deals primarily with Goethe, provides some valuable suggestions. Preisendanz sees in the epigram the stylistic expression of the Renaissance ideal of elegance and the natural outgrowth of a humanistic outlook

---

[10] See for example Heinrich Denker, *Ein Beitrag zur litterarischen Würdigung Friedrichs von Logau* (diss., Göttingen, 1889) (hereafter cited as *Logau*). The only book-length study of Logau is Paul Hempel, *Die Kunst Friedrichs von Logau,* Palaestra, vol. 130 (Berlin, 1917).

[11] In Göteborg Högskolas årsskrift, vol. 55 (Göteborg, 1949); recently translated into German, "Die Motive und Tendenzen des deutschen Epigramms im 17. Jahrhundert," in *Das Epigramm. Zur Geschichte einer inschriftlichen und literarischen Gattung,* ed. Gerhard Pfohl (Darmstadt, 1969), pp. 287-351 (hereafter cited as *Das Epigramm*). The Reclam anthology *Deutsche Epigramme,* ed. Gerhard Neumann (Stuttgart, 1969) makes use of some of my findings, including selections from the epigrams of Ambrosius Lobwasser to whose importance my dissertation (Berkeley, 1967) first drew attention. Mr. Neumann acknowledges this debt in his "Nachwort," pp. 294 and 357. The most recent contribution to the subject is Günther C. Rimbach, "Das Epigramm und die Barockpoetik," *Jahrbuch der deutschen Schillergesellschaft* 14 (1970): 100-31. It appeared while this study was in press.

[12] "Dagegen muß es im Jahre 1949 ein wenig überraschen, daß die moderne geistesgeschichtliche deutsche (und nicht-deutsche) Forschung diesem Gelehrten fremd geblieben ist." Erik Lunding, "Stand und Aufgaben der deutschen Barockforschung," *Orbis Litterarum* 8 (1950): 51.

on life. [13] In this he follows the general guidelines spelled out by Paul Böckmann. [14]

Not only is there a dearth of critical material, but the texts themselves are hard to come by. Even Logau, the most eminent of the secular epigrammatists, has not been republished since 1872. [15] Sometimes not even a collected edition will insure the inclusion of a poet's epigrams in their entirety. Thus Werner Milch, Czepko's editor, omitted about half of Czepko's secular epigrams from his edition of the poet's *Weltliche Dichtungen* (Breslau, 1932). Poets of lesser rank can often be found only in anthologies if the original editions are not available. Furthermore, a number of epigrammatists have probably dropped from sight. A case in point is Ambrosius Lobwasser's *Epigrammata,* a book of considerable significance that is virtually unknown.

Considering how little work has been done on the subject, the present study cannot aim to be either exhaustive or conclusive. What seemed needed was an overall interpretative view and an introduction to the variety of epigrammatic practice. These I have tried to provide. One of my aims is to contribute to the under-standing of Baroque poetry through the examination of one of its genres, and another is to shed more light on the genre of the epigram by examining it in one of its strongest periods. More specifically, this study deals with the connection between classical and indigenous elements in the epigram; it reexamines the begin-nings of consciously epigrammatic writing in German and traces them back to the sixteenth century; it places popular inscriptions and the religious epigram within an epigrammatic context. Viewing these forms within a wider context and in relation to one another has produced a new perspective and hence some new conclusions.

---

[13] Preisendanz, *Spruchform,* pp. 30-31.

[14] Paul Böckmann, *Formgeschichte der deutschen Dichtung* (Hamburg, 1965), 1:318-471.

[15] *Friedrichs von Logau sämmtliche Sinngedichte,* ed. Gustav Eitner, Bibliothek des Litterarischen Vereins in Stuttgart, vol. 113 (Tubingen, 1872). The *Sinngedichte* are arranged in groups of one thousand. These, in turn, are subdivided by hundreds. The second and third thousand are followed by what Logau called a *Zu-Gabe* of 201 and 257 verses respectively. In my citations I follow Eitner in designating each thousand by a Roman numeral, the hundreds and singles by arabic numerals. *Z* stands for the *Zu-Gabe* following the second thousand, *ZD* for the *Zu-Gabe* following the third thousand.

The material exists in enormous quantity, frequently unedited, and in unwieldy form. A considerable sampling of epigrams that seemed to have either historical significance or poetic merit are analyzed, although it is not my primary intention to study individual epigrammatists but rather to choose what is either representative or outstanding. The work of Logau, for example, will be found in a variety of contexts, since he is admirably suitable on both counts.

I have concluded with two questions: What can be accomplished by a poem that is as self-limiting as the epigram? And what was actually accomplished by the epigram in the seventeenth century?

CHAPTER I

THE EPIGRAM AS A GENRE

To THE GENERAL READER NOWADAYS *epigram* MEANS A SHORT, witty poem. However, as soon as one examines any of the periods in which the genre flourished, it becomes apparent that such a definition does not cover nearly enough ground. Epigrams have been written on every conceivable subject and in every variety of mood and timbre. As a result the epigram on second thought is frequently defined very comprehensively. The definition in the *Encyclopaedia Britannica* states: "The epigram is one of the most catholic of literary forms, and lends itself to the expression of almost any thought or feeling. It may be an elegy, a satire or a lovepoem in miniature, an embodiment of the wisdom of the ages, a bon-mot set off with a couple of rhymes." One scholar, trying to accommodate both views, assigned to the witty type a central position, stating that it was the "most epigrammatic of epigrams." He continued: "We might say that other varieties grade down from it: on the one side in the direction of the maxim, proverb, or gnomic verse ...; on another side in the direction of the lyric ...; on another side in the direction of the satirical essay ...; on another side in the direction of the verse-epistle or the elegy ...; while in epitaphs and funereal epigrams the tendency is toward the dirge or threnody." [1] This catalog is impressive and, moreover, correct. However, the implicit metaphor of a pyramid with the various types scaling down from the satirical epigram suggests a relation of

---

[1] Hoyt Hopewell Hudson, *The Epigram in the English Renaissance* (Princeton, N. J., 1947), p. 13 (hereafter cited as *The Epigram*).

dependence that does not exist. And it obscures the fact that there actually are two recognizable trends in epigrammatic writing: one toward the simple lyric and the other toward the bipartite verse aphorism. Seen from another angle, this is the distinction between the naive and the pointed epigram or, in historical perspective, the distinction between the typical Greek and the typical Latin epigram.

The word *epigram* itself means inscription (from Greek ἐπιγράφειν, "to write upon"). The earliest epigrams were inscriptions on tombstones, monuments, houses, gifts, or sacrificial offerings. Most of the epigrams in the *Greek Anthology,* the earliest written collection of epigrams, are of this kind, although many were written as literary exercises, that is, for their own sake and not for any practical purpose. Yet the original purpose of the epigram never disappeared completely and continued to affect the development of the genre. For example, in seventeenth-century Germany one type of inscription, the epitaph, became a highly developed, richly sophisticated, and much practiced literary exercise. A century later Schiller's and Goethe's *Xenien* pretended, like Martial's, to be inscribed on party gifts. In the twentieth century Stefan George, recalling the origin of the term, called his epigrams *Tafeln.* [2]

The *Greek Anthology* became known in Italy in the late fifteenth century and gained currency throughout Europe during the sixteenth, when the writing of epigrams was becoming fashionable among the educated. These epigrammatists modeled their products after either the Greeks or the Romans and wrote first in Latin but later in the vernacular languages of their respective countries. Most of the verses in the *Greek Anthology* are lyrics; that is, they are not primarily witty, and only a few are satirical. [3] Rarely do they make the lucid appeal to the conscious mind which is characteristic of the later, pointed epigram. They deal largely with the emotions, and their appeal is through various levels of association, both linguistic and metaphorical, as is the case with other lyric poems. Here is an example by Kallimachos (8.453):

[2] Stefan George, *Werke* (Munich, 1958), pp. 324-42.
[3] See Franz Josef Brecht, "Motiv- und Typengeschichte des griechischen Spottepigramms," *Philologus,* suppl. vol. 22, part 2 (1930): 1-114 passim.

> His father Philip laid here his twelve-year old boy
> Nikoteles:
>> his dearest hope. [4]

The poem describes a simple, specific, unified situation. It consists of one element only, the death of a child survived by his father. It is highly charged with emotion, but its restrained grief is tersely expressed.

An epigram by Martial may serve as a contrast. Martial has been called "der Klassiker des abendländischen Epigramms," and he was for a long time thought to have been the originator of the pointed epigram. [5] The example chosen is the same length as the epigram by Kallimachos and it, too, deals with the death of a particular person:

> Hostem cum fugeret, se Fannius ipse peremit.
> Hic, rogo, non furor est, ne moriare, mori?
>> (2. 80)

In the first line a fugitive kills himself. But where the second line of the Greek epigram continues without a change of outlook and is expressive of grief, Martial moves from the specific to the general and engages the reader in an abstract reflection on the absurdity of a man's inflicting death on himself in order to escape death. By way of reenforcing the paradox, the poet plays with the modes of "to die," placing "moriare, mori" in adjacent positions. In the death of Fannius the author seeks to gain the reader's assent to the reflection he has advanced. The death of Nikoteles, on the other hand, is meant to engage the reader's sympathy and move him to share the father's loss.

---

[4] English version by Dudley Fitts, *Poems from the Greek Anthology in English Paraphrase* (New York, 1956), p. 109.

[5] The question of what Martial actually does owe to the Greeks need not detain us here. What matters is that for the entire period under consideration, and for a long time afterwards, his work was considered both the first and the best of its kind. See Otto Seel, "Ansatz zu einer Martial-Interpretation," in Pfohl, *Das Epigramm,* pp. 153-86. Seel writes: "Gewiß steht Martial in einer Tradition, und er selbst war sich dessen sehr wohl bewußt. Aber gewirkt hat er so, als wäre er der Erfinder und Begründer dieses Spieles mit spitzen Worten" (p. 162).

German criticism possesses two penetrating essays, one by Lessing and another by Herder, on the nature of the epigram. There is no better introduction to the subject than a close examination of these two pieces. Lessing's essay, "Zerstreute Anmerkungen über das Epigramm und einige der vornehmsten Epigrammatisten," is quite systematic despite its unassuming title. [6] Its great merit lies in the discernment of the connection between the naive inscription and the complex, pointed epigram of later times. Lessing attacked his problem with characteristic directness by asking: "Was hat das witzigste Sinngedicht eines Martial mit der trockensten Aufschrift eines alten Denkmals gemein, so dass beide bei einem Volke, dessen Sprache wohl am wenigsten unter allen Sprachen dem Zufalle überlassen war, einerlei Namen führen konnten?" The inscription on the monument, he answered, is designed to satisfy the spectator's curiosity, which has been aroused by the monument itself. Such a description will be plain, forthright, and informative. But in its subtler and more artistic form, the first part of the epigram must fulfill the monument's function. The epigram rises to the level of poetry only when it is not the adjunct of a physical object, but provides a verbal symbol. Having excited the reader's curiosity in its first part, the epigram will then satisfy this curiosity in its second part. Hence all true epigrams are bipartite. Lessing called the two parts Erwartung, "anticipation," and Aufschluss "resolution." (In some cases "exposition" may be a better translation than the more literal "anticipation"; Lessing's meaning falls somewhere between the two.)

It had long been recognized that an epigram could have either a simple or a bipartite structure. Scaliger, whom Lessing quoted, had spoken of the difference in his *Poetices Libri Septes* of 1561: "Epigramma igitur est poema breve cum simplici cuiuspliam rei, vel personae, vel facti indicatione, aut ex propositis aliquid deducens." But Lessing was the first to see the intrinsic connection between the two types and to evaluate them. He took issue with anyone like Scaliger and Batteux who had granted literary recognition to the simpler type, for he insisted on the quality of pointedness

---

[6] Gotthold Ephraim Lessing, *Lessings Werke*, ed. Julius Petersen and Waldemar von Olshausen (Leipzig, n. d.), 14: 118-208 (hereafter cited as *Werke*).

as one of the hallmarks of the epigram. [7] However, he was careful to state that a mere witticism would not do. The second part, the resolution, must contain precisely the idea for which the epigram was written and our expectation was aroused in the first place. But neither is an interesting idea by itself enough to make an epigram, according to Lessing. That would be the resolution without the anticipation, the comment without the object to which the comment applies; it would be the equivalent of the inscription without the monument.

Lessing's theory retains the original meaning of the term *epigram*, which was based on the original function of the poem. The composite epigram emerges as a natural development of the simple inscription, the epigraph. Lessing took into account the unusual degree to which the epigram is "objective" in the literal sense of being object-oriented. (A better term is the German *gegenstandsbezogen*.) He examined the epigram as the poem of the observed world, specific and geared to reality.

The weakness of Lessing's essay lies in his uncompromising rejection of the simple epigram and his insistence that all true epigrams must be both witty and bipartite. (We shall see that Herder took an almost opposite view.) It is possible to see Lessing's bias as a rationalized, "enlightened" misreading of the profound ambiguities that lie at the heart of Baroque antithesis. Antithesis is not a necessary ingredient of epigrammatic art; it is, however, a characteristic ingredient of Baroque epigrammatic art. Lessing, it will be remembered, edited Logau, admired Wernicke, and was himself a late practitioner of the art of the elegant epigram. The polemicist in him must have been attracted to the antithetical nature of the epigram as he found it. But because he belonged to a more rational age, the troubled wellspring of Baroque antithesis escaped him. He saw it as "Erwartung und Aufschluss," whereas the Baroque poet would often present insoluble contradictions in his bipartite structure.

Lessing's essay was first published in volume one of his *Vermischte Schriften* of 1771. It was reviewed by Herder in the

---

[7] This quality also went by such names as *argutia, acumen, Spitzfindigkeit*. For a detailed study of this concept, see Therese Erb, *Die Pointe in der Dichtung von Barock und Aufklärung* (Bonn, 1929).

Allgemeine Deutsche Bibliothek. [8] Herder recognized that here, for the first time, was a theory that explained the epigram according to laws of its own. At the same time he was not satisfied, for he came to the subject as an enthusiastic student of the *Greek Anthology* and with a hearty dislike for the later, pointed epigram. "Vielleicht ists bei mir eben auch Einseitigkeit des Geschmacks," he wrote to Hamann, "daß ich die Spitzen des Martialischen Sinn- und Windgedichts nie habe lieben können und mich an einer sim- plen Viole oder Rose im griechischen Geschmack immer mehr erquickte." [9]

In 1785 Herder expounded his own views in an essay entitled "Anmerkungen über das griechische Epigram." [10] The basic epigram, he stated, was exposition pure and simple, "die einfache und darstellende Form des Epigramms." [11] Here there is no disagreement with Lessing. But, Herder continued, not only was this the basic type of epigram, it was also the best type. "Ich bekenne aber, daß manche dieser simplen Expositionen für mich viel mehr Rührendes und Reizendes haben, als die geschraubte epigrammatische Spitz- fündigkeit späterer Zeiten." And again: "Was fehlt diesen Zuschrif- ten an Kürze, Würde und rührender Einfalt? Wem sie mit ihrer simpeln Exposition nichts sagen: was werden sie ihm durch vieles Wortgepränge zu sagen vermögen?" [12] The key word in these two passages is "rührend." Herder expected to be moved by the epigram as he would expect a lyric poem (but not a maxim or an aphorism) to move him; that is, the pleasure to be had from the epigram was not primarily an intellectual but rather an emotional satisfaction. In this respect Herder's essay differs radically from any previous criticism of the epigram, reestablishing the epigram as a lyric form by demanding that the reader react to it as he would to any other lyric.

---

[8] Ernst Beutler, *Vom griechischen Epigramm im 18. Jahrhundert,* Probe- fahrten, vol. 15 (Leipzig, 1909), pp. 53-54; partially reprinted in Pfohl, *Das Epigramm,* pp. 353-416.

[9] Beutler, *Vom griechischen Epigramm,* p. 58.

[10] Johann Gottfried Herder, *Herders Sämmtliche Werke,* ed. Bernhard Suphan (Berlin, 1888), 15: 337-92.

[11] Ibid., p. 355.

[12] Ibid., pp. 348, 351.

Lessing and Herder together admirably summed up the scope and limits of the epigram: Lessing stressed its bipartite aspect, Herder, its unity. Where Lessing inclined toward pointedness or *argutia,* Herder extolled simplicity. Lessing's model was Martial; Herder's was the *Greek Anthology.* Herder praised the lyrical qualities of the epigram, while Lessing was more attracted by its appeal to the intellect. Both views are correct. Even the poems in the *Greek Anthology,* for all their emotional and musical qualities, have a subdued aphoristic tendency which is perhaps inherent in the single or double distich. It may be objected that the two trends are incompatible, that the aphoristic and the lyrical tendency cannot peacefully coexist. The objection is justified to the extent that the epigram does indeed occupy a border position among lyrics. The epigram is the lyric that bridges the gap between a poetic and a prose statement, inclining toward reason even when it is used as a vehicle for mysticism (in the sense that it is used only as an expression of *Verstandesmystik,* not *Gefühlsmystik*). Much of its charm depends on the tension between these conflicting elements. This is particularly apparent in the seventeenth century, when *ratio* played a much clearer role in all types of poetry than it did in later periods.

The simple and the bipartite structures comprise the two basic types of epigrams. Any structure that involves more than two major elements is ipso facto not epigrammatic. Hence an epigram will usually have only one stanza, though examples of two occur. But any poem with three or more stanzas follows a strophic organization which is intrinsically too complex for the epigram. By the same rule one may say, although with some hesitation, that a good epigram should not exceed twelve lines, two lines less than a sonnet. A longer poem has of necessity a structural variety that precludes the epigrammatic effect. Sonnets and longer poems may have epigrammatic endings, but they cannot in themselves be epigrams because of their more complex organization.

Since it is a lyric poem, narrative and dramatic elements are essentially alien to the epigram. Short rhymed anecdotes are not uncommon in epigram collections, but these must be judged misplaced fables or hybrids between the fable and the epigram. Similarly, brief epigrammatic dialogues are departures from the norm, but it is not surprising that the antithetical nature of the epigram caused some poets to introduce dialogue. As for the "inscriptive" qualities that Lessing stressed, it is always correct to think of the epigram as an unusually concrete poem elucidating the fragment of reality on which it is "engraved."

What was the relative prevalence of the lyric and the pointed epigram during the Renaissance and afterward? German scholars tend to give Herder credit for discovering the lyrical potential of the epigram in his studies of the *Greek Anthology*. Yet James Hutton has shown in two admirable volumes that the epigram of the Greek type was highly influential and widely practiced in Italy and France. [13] Hutton writes: "It cannot be too much emphasized that this epigram, written by the Italian and French Latinists of the Renaissance, was not the sharp-pointed and mainly satirical type which since the seventeenth century has been primarily suggested by the term. ... More often and more characteristically... [it dealt with] themes of love, of nature, of honor, of sorrow — in a word, all the topics of poetry!" [14] Each of the European languages had its own small poetic forms — for example, *dizain* and *huitain* in France, sonnet and madrigal in Italy — and when the *Anthology* first became known, Italian and French poets began to compare the epigram with their indigenous small forms and developed "the doctrine of equivalence of forms, whereby it was asserted that the sonnet (sometimes the madrigal) takes in Italian the place of the epigram in Greek." [15] As early as 1548, Sebillet had written in his *Poétique*: "Sonnet n'est autre chose que le parfait épigramme de l'Italien." [16] Sonnets were written on themes from Greek epigrams and, according to Hutton, the epigram probably caused a modification in the structure of the sonnet, culminating in the so-called Shakespearean sonnet with the epigrammatic couplet at the end. [17]

---

[13] James Hutton, *The Greek Anthology in Italy to the Year 1800*, Cornell Studies in English, vol. 23 (Ithaca, N. Y., 1935); James Hutton, *The Greek Anthology in France*, Cornell Studies in Classical Philology, vol. 28 (Ithaca, N. Y., 1946).

[14] Hutton, *Greek Anthology in France*, p. 34.

[15] Hutton, *Greek Anthology in Italy*, p. 50.

[16] Ibid., p. 56.

[17] Hutton's work is apparently not well known among German scholars. Werner Mönch not only ignores the epigrammatic influence on the sonnet

In Germany critics favored the satirical epigram, but poets long persisted in associating the epigram with other lyrical short forms. Zincgref's edition of Opitz's *Teutsche Poemata* of 1624 contains a number of poems by Opitz and others which are called epigrams but are really songs, sonnets, and other lyric forms. Among Gryphius's epigrams are a number of poems that approximate the sonnet structure but fall short by two or four lines, giving us the impression that he considered a defective sonnet to be an epigram. Scheffler included twelve sonnets in *Der Cherubinische Wandersmann,* [18] and Czepko introduced each book of his *Monodisticha* with a sonnet which he called *Klingel,* no doubt after the etymology of *sonnet* from *sonner,* mentioned by Opitz. [19] *Schlußreime,* a frequent term for epigrams, suggests a connection with longer lyric forms. In addition, almost all the song writers of the age were also expert epigrammatists, as a glance at the index of Günther Müller's *Geschichte des deutschen Liedes* (Munich, 1925) will indicate. The lyric approach accounts for the fact that the epigram was considered suitable for religious purposes. This background also accounts to a great extent for the prevailing concern with form and language among the epigrammatists of the period. To be sure, this is a characteristically Baroque concern, but it is nevertheless surprising to find it in the epigram, which was a rather umpromising form for technical experimentation since its brevity severely limited the range and freedom of the poet.

In poetics, on the other hand, the notion that the epigram should be satirical predominated, beginning with Opitz's definition in his *Buch von der deutschen Poeterey:*

Das Epigramma setze ich darumb zue der Satyra/ weil die Satyra ein lang Epigramma/ vnd das Epigramma eine kurtze Satyra ist: denn die kürtze ist seine eigenschafft/ vnd die spitzfindigkeit gleichsam seine seele vnd gestalt; die sonderlich an dem ende erscheinet/ das allezeit anders als wir verhoffet hetten gefallen soll: in welchem auch die spitzfindigkeit vornemlich bestehet. [20]

---

but is also unaware of the fact that the "Shakespearean" sonnet was an Italian, not an English, invention. Werner Mönch, *Das Sonett. Gestalt und Geschichte* (Heidelberg, 1955), p. 19.

[18] At the beginning of the sixth book.

[19] Martin Opitz, *Buch von der deutschen Poeterey (1624),* Neudrucke deutscher Literaturwerke, new ser., vol. 8, ed. Wilhelm Braune and Richard Alewyn (Tubingen, 1963), p. 41 (hereafter cited as *Poeterey*).

Later theorists followed this definition with little or no variation virtually up to the time of Lessing. Their consensus has been noted by several critics, most recently Preisendanz, who writes: "So dürftig diese Charakteristik anmuten kann, so bindend blieb sie für das Jahrhundert, so ausreichend muss sie also gewesen sein." [21]

The lines just quoted are only the beginning of Opitz's definition, which is not altogether "dürftig." Opitz's contemporaries and later critics focused their attention on this passage because it is both lucid and simple. But Opitz continued:

Wiwol aber das Epigramma aller sachen vnnd wörter fähig ist/ sol es doch lieber in Venerischem wesen/ vberschrifften der begräbnisse vnd gebäwe/ Lobe vornemer Männer vnd Frawen/ kurtzweiligen schertzreden vnnd anderem/ es sey was es wolle/ bestehen/ als in spöttlicher hönerey vnd auffruck anderer leute laster vnd gebrechen. Denn es ist eine anzeignung eines unverschämten sicheren gemütes/ einen ietwedern/ wie unvernünfftige thiere thun/ ohne vnterscheidt anlauffen. [22]

It is apparent that his full definition is riddled with ambiguities. He stated in the first part that the epigram should be a satire, yet he proceeded to insist that it be a love poem, a house or tomb inscription, in fact anything but a satire, if the satire was offensive. Significantly, in his last sentence Opitz argued not from a literary point of view but from the point of view of the whole man: To offend others by mocking them shows bad character and is beastlike behavior. Here the Renaissance idea that a man's writing reflects his character — a notion quite distinct from the eighteenth-century idea that it should reflect his experience — is still in full force. Opitz's definition of the epigram, in spite of its dogmatic beginning, belongs to a period that was not yet fully convinced of the preeminence of the satirical epigram but retained an interest in the capacity for variety of the small forms. The definition is as Janus-faced as

---

[20] Ibid., p. 21.

[21] Preisendanz, *Spruchform*, p. 30. He cites Jakob Masen, Schottel, Kaspar Ziegler, and others in evidence. The history of epigrammatic theory has been treated in some detail by Rudolf Pechel as part of his edition of Wernicke's works. Christian Wernicke, *Christian Wernicke's Epigramme*, ed. Rudolf Pechel, Palaestra, vol. 81 (Berlin, 1909), pp. 1-23 (hereafter cited as *Epigramme*). See also Bruno Markwardt, *Geschichte der deutschen Poetik*, vol. 1 (Berlin, 1937).

[22] Opitz, *Poeterey*, p. 21.

anything Opitz produced: he was establishing standards that were accepted into the Enlightenment, and yet he was working within a Renaissance tradition. This frame of mind seems to have been so natural to him that he was unaware of the self-contradictory aspects of his definition.

It is a common fallacy to assume that the modern European epigram must be Greek in origin because the oldest epigram collection is the *Anthology*. [23] This error arises when the nonclassical sources of the vernacular epigram are ignored. As a matter of fact, a tradition of poetic inscriptions was likely to spring up quite independently, as it did in Germany, wherever literate communities existed. Robert Petsch says quite correctly: "Der kurzen, inhaltreichen, aufweckenden und oft verblüffenden Art des 'Epigramms' bei den Alten entspricht genau die Art unserer 'Inschrift,' wie sie der Bauer so gern an der Außenwand seines Hauses, an den Balken, an den Schränken und vor allem an den Ess- und Trinkgeräten anbringt." [24] Even a hundred years ago L. Forck recognized this when he subtitled his collection of popular inscriptions *zur epigrammatischen Volkspoesie,* following J. v. Radowitz's reference to *Volksepigramme*. [25] But the connection seems apparent only to those who approach the subject from the folkloristic point of view. It has had no effect on discussions of the literary German epigram. Indeed, criticism of the epigram provides an illustration of the fact that a narrow definition is not always precise. The indigenous small forms in Germany, less elaborate than their Romance counterparts, are usually summed up by the term *Spruch*. The term "epigram" was not used until the sixteenth or seventeenth century. But the thing itself existed in one form or another, and when we are dealing with poems written after the foreign word became current, it becomes difficult, it not impossible, to distinguish between epigram and *Spruch*. German scholars are misleading in their frequent insistence

---

[23] Two recent examples of this assumption are Werner Peek in the preface to *Griechische Grabgedichte. Griechisch und deutsch,* Schriften und Quellen der alten Welt, vol. 7 (Berlin, 1960); and Pfohl, *Das Epigramm,* p. 8.

[24] Robert Petsch, *Spruchdichtung des Volkes* (Halle, 1938), p. 128 (hereafter cited as *Spruchdichtung*).

[25] L. Forck, *Deutsche Inschriften an Haus und Geräth* (Berlin, 1865) (hereafter cited as *Deutsche Inschriften*). Forck quotes Radowitz, the editor of a medieval collection, on p. v.

on separating the two into distinct and mutually exclusive genres. Confusion exists even in standard works such as the Merker-Stammler *Reallexikon*, [26] which states that during the Middle Ages the epigram was practiced in Latin but not in German. As examples of medieval epigrams the *Reallexikon* cites Latin inscriptions on houses, pictures, and household utensils, but it fails to mention that such inscriptions were composed in German as well, mostly anonymously, but sometimes by poets such as Spervogel. If these inscriptions are not considered epigrams because they are in German, then the *Reallexikon*'s statement that only Latin epigrams were written in the Middle Ages is based on a circuitous argument. Similarly, the seventeenth-century epigram is often severely censured for its alleged lack of originality and spontaneity. Yet whenever a short poem is an original verse in the vernacular rather than a derivation from Greek or Latin, it is not classed as an epigram but as a *Spruch*. Thus the form is condemned as derivative after it has been defined as derivative. This is similar to the problem Hudson points out from the English point of view: "To put the matter bluntly, the moment an epigram becomes very good... it is in danger of being classed as a lyric." [27]

A historical examination shows that the medieval *Spruch* received a new impetus and a new direction under the influence of the humanist-inspired rediscovery of the classical small forms. From an etymological point of view, both *Spruch* and *Sprichwort* imply an oral tradition, while "epigram" and its many seventeenth-century equivalents in German, such as *Beyschrifft, Auffschrifft,* and *Überschrifft,* imply a written tradition. This etymological distinction, though attractive, is unsound when we consider that Logau's seventeenth-century epigrams employed almost as much folklore as Freidank's thirteenth-century *Sprüche*. Both drew heavily, but by no means exclusively, on popular or proverbial wisdom. Moreover, in the sixteenth and seventeenth centuries, when the Neo-Latin epigrams of the Humanists were first rendered into the modern European languages, the distinction between written and oral tradi-

---

[26] Paul Merker and Wolfgang Stammler, *Reallexikon der deutschen Literaturgeschichte,* 2d ed. (Berlin, 1964) 1: 374 (hereafter cited as *Reallexikon*).

[27] Hudson, *The Epigram,* pp. 7-8.

tions was becoming increasingly blurred because of the expanding use of the printing press and the attendant increase in literacy. Classical quotes were becoming proverbial, while proverbs and other indigenous material were being collected and published. This development deserves closer attention.

The rise of the German epigram in the seventeenth century was by no means an isolated phenomenon but rather part of a generally increasing interest in the small forms of poetry. The Humanists' accumulation of encyclopedic knowledge seems to have had its counterpart in a desire to express wisdom in short and pithy sayings, to make it memorable by compressing much meaning into few words. Both trends started in the Renaissance and continued through the seventeenth century.

Collections of small forms of various kinds and origins were very popular. There were, for example, sayings and quotations from the ancients, detached from their original context. The most famous and influential collection of this sort was Erasmus's *Adagia,* which appeared in several successive editions during his lifetime, each one enlarged; the last one, published in 1536, the year of their compiler's death, contained four thousand items. This book "became the commonplace book, *par excellence,* from which everyone, including Luther himself, drew his classical quotations." [28] It was imitated throughout the sixteenth and seventeenth centuries. At the same time a number of German proverb collections appeared, beginning with Johann Agricola's collection, first published in Magdeburg in 1528, then in Eisleben in 1548, and again in Wittenberg in 1592. [29] It was perhaps no accident that it was published there, for Agricola belonged to Luther's circle, and Luther himself not only collected proverbs [30] but also put them to use, for example, by ending his fables with a series of proverbs rather than a moral. [31] Later reformers developed the art of the pithy saying into the weapon of the polemical epigram.

What did the early proverb collections contain? We expect a proverb to make a point, but originally this was not necessarily

---

[28] Henry Osborn Taylor, *Erasmus and Luther* (New York, 1962), p. 44.
[29] For exact bibliographical data on proverb collections, see Otto E. Möll, *Sprichwörter-Bibliographie* (Frankfort, 1958), which supersedes Wilfrid Bonser, *Proverb Literature: A Bibliography* (London, 1930).
[30] *Luthers Sprichwörtersammlung,* ed. Ernst Otto Thiele (Weimar, 1900).
[31] Friedrich Seiler, *Sprichwörterkunde* (Munich, 1922), p. 116.

one of its characteristics. Both the proverb and the epigram became more pointed in the later sixteenth and the seventeenth centuries. At first a *Sprichwort* could be simply a common saying, a turn of phrase, or a metaphor. The Eisleben edition of the Agricola collection contains many sayings such as "weyss wie eine Kreyde, schwartz wie die erde, blawe wie der Himmel" (nos. 599-601) and "Es gehet zu, wie in König Artus hofe" (no. 668), as well as greetings (nos. 544-49) and curses (nos. 472-501).[32] They are imaginative, and their editor may have deliberately increased their effectiveness by his artful arrangement: "Das dich die Pestilentz ankomme" (no. 476) is followed by "Das dich die Frantzosen ankommen" (no. 477), perhaps with the intention of adding insult to injury. A few proverbs are actually epigrammatic. Number 32 is quite polished and shows a complex humor:

> Wer will haben ein reynes hauss,
> Der lass Pfaffen, Münch und tauben drauss.

In this verse simple enumeration creates an implied *tertium comparationis* between clergymen and pigeons, thus equating immorality with dirt. The same technique of insult through association may be observed in Logau's very similar, though much later, epigram:

> Stinkend Käs und Wahrheit
> Liegt bei Höfen abseit.
> (III, 1, 11)

The loose juxtaposition turns the rotten cheese more effectively into a symbol of truth than a direct simile could. Nothing further need be said about the courts wanting the latter as little as if it were the former. These verses go even further than Heine's famous and much admired linking of Göttingen's sausages and its university.

These two examples show how a rhymed and pointed proverb is virtually indistinguishable from an epigram. André Jolles makes the same claim of concreteness for the proverb that we have been making for the epigram: "Die Sprache des Sprichwortes ist so, dass alle seine Teile einzeln, in ihrer Bedeutung, in ihren syntakti-

---

[32] Reprinted in Felix Bobertag, ed., *Volksbücher des 16. Jahrhunderts,* Deutsche National Literatur, vol. 25 (Berlin, n.d.), pp. 411-32.

schen und stilistischen Bindungen, in ihrer klanglichen Bewegung in Abwehr gegen jede Verallgemeinerung und jede Abstraktion stehen." [33] Proverb and epigram are very close relatives indeed. At first sight the differences may be striking: the proverb apparently has no classical pretensions, it is anonymous and widely known among the illiterate, and it reaches far back into the past. Yet actually the origins of the German *Sprichwort* are often not ancient; they are merely obscure. [34] On the whole, German proverbs are a development of the fifteenth and sixteenth centuries, and while some of them may derive from medieval *Sprüche,* the same claim can be made for many epigrams. Seiler's investigations have shown that fewer proverbs are of medieval origin than one would suspect, that many of them owe much to Latin antecedents — just as many epigrams do — and that some occur for the first time at the end of the six-teenth century. [35] Moreover, the poets were encouraged to use proverbs as a source for epigrams. For example, in 1682 Daniel Georg Morhof devoted several pages of his *Unterricht von der teutschen Sprache und Poesie* to explaining and exemplifying "wie nützlich man dergleichen Sprüchwörter gebrauchen könne... wesshalben ich jederzeit zu rahten pflege / dass man die *Adagia* und *Adagialia,* aus aller Art *Autoribus* und Sprachen / unter gewissen Titel zusammen lesen solle. ... Es ist nicht zu gläuben / was dieses zu Erfindungen nütze." [36] He gave examples and praised the authors of prose proverbs that had been expanded and put into verse.

The connection between proverb and epigram is further confirmed by their use in the schools. Proverbs were widely used as topics for themes. [37] The epigram was employed in a similar although somewhat more elaborate way. In the Humanist schools it was customary to give the students an epigram in either Greek or Latin and have them restate it, apply it, or comment on it. [38] The first of these exercises might involve the writing of new although unoriginal epigrams. Imitating the Humanists, the Jesuit schools made epigram

[33] André Jolles, *Einfache Formen* (Halle, 1956), p. 137.
[34] Ibid., pp. 124-27; Seiler, *Sprichwörterkunde,* chap. 2, passim.
[35] Seiler, *Sprichwörterkunde,* p. 25.
[36] Daniel Georg Morhof, *Unterricht von der teutschen Sprache und Poesie,* 3d ed. (Leipzig, 1718), pp. 687-91.
[37] Seiler, *Sprichwörterkunde,* chap. 14, passim.
[38] Hudson, *The Epigram,* chap. 4, passim.

writing a regular part of the curriculum. Their handbook, *Ratio atque institutio studiorum societatis Jesu,* published in Antwerp in 1635, suggested that "while the master is correcting papers, his pupils may spend the time imitating a passage from a poet or an orator, in varying the same sentence in many ways, in turning one kind of poem into another, or in writing epigrams, inscriptions and epitaphs. In his Greek prelections the master may once a week introduce a few epigrams." [39]

The same age that saw the rise of the proverb collections and the beginnings of epigrammatic writing also ushered in the *Stammbuch,* the album in which friends wrote memorable sayings or verses for one another. [40] The custom was then current chiefly among university students, the same group that had been trained as boys in school to comment on German proverbs and to turn one Latin epigram into another Latin epigram. Originally the *Stammbuchvers* was a heraldic inscription, an explanation in verse of a heraldic design. Later one could buy books especially designed as *Stammbücher* containing blank heraldic devices to be filled in as well as Latin and German verses to choose from. The title of one of these runs in full: "Stamm oder Gesellenbuch. Mit vil schönen Sprüchen, auch allerley offnen vnd Bürgerlichen Schildten vnd Helmen. Allen Studenten vnd sonst guten Gesellen, so entweder jre Wapen, Reimen oder Sprüch zur gedechtnuss einander verlassen wöllten, zu dienst vnd gefallen zusammen getragen, 1574." [41] The many published collections of proverbs, epigrams, and maxims furnished an inexhaustible store of verses for those who were too unimaginative to make up their own. Verses specifically written for a *Stammbuch* can be found in the works (often the epigrams) of some of the most prominent Baroque poets, including Gryphius and Czepko. [42]

Essentially the *Stammbuchvers* was nothing but an application of a proverb or an epigram. It is therefore hardly surprising that the

---

[39] Quoted by Hutton, *Greek Anthology in Italy,* p. 44.

[40] Robert and Richard Keil, *Die deutschen Stammbücher des sechzehnten bis neunzehnten Jahrhunderts* (Berlin, 1893) (hereafter cited as *Deutsche Stammbücher*).

[41] Ibid., pp. 28-29.

[42] See for example Daniel von Czepko, *Weltliche Dichtungen,* ed. Werner Milch (Breslau, 1932), p. 426.

first ones were written mainly in Latin and that the early German
ones strongly resemble the proverbs in collections:

> Ein Schneider auf eim Ross
> Ein Hur aufm Schloss
> Ein Lauss auf dem Grind
> Seyn drey stolze Hofgesind.

(1556)

Later there are lampoons on proverbs, which is a natural development, considering the students' school experience with themes:

> Ehrlich vnd fromm werdt am Längsten   (werdt = währt)
> Dan man braucht es am wengsten.

(1624)

Nor did they spare their universities:

> Wer auss Jena kombt ungeschlagen,
> Der kann von grossem Glücke sagen

(1678)

against *à la mode*:

> Ich bin kein schifflein auf der See,
> Dass nach des Windes Wellen geh,
> Ich liebe mit bestendigkeit
> Die alte deutsche Redligkeit

(1639)

and the opposed, cosmopolitan view:

> Wer allzeit bei dem Ofen sitzt,
> Grillen und die Höltzlein spitzt,
> Vnd frembde lande nicht beschawt,
> Der ist ein Aff in seiner Haut. [43]

(1648)

The main concern here is to show how widespread, popular, and
varied epigrammatic writing was and how closely the different types
were related. The *Stammbuchvers* was based on both German

---

[43] Keil and Keil, *Deutsche Stammbücher,* pp. 93, 116, 142, 111, 109.

proverbs and Latin school learning, but it also touched the most eccentric branch of epigrammatic writing, the emblem book. Emblem books were frequently used as *Stammbücher,* with blank sheets inserted between the printed pages for handwritten additions.

In the emblem books an obscure picture was interpreted symbolically by means of an epigram called a *subscriptio.* Harsdörffer called the picture *Sinnbild,* [44] a name obviously connected with *Sinngedicht,* the most common German term for epigram. Just as the original epigraph or inscription depended on a physical object for its very existence, so the *subscriptio* of the emblem depended wholly on a picture, a visible object one step removed from reality; the *subscriptio* tended to interpret the image in an unexpected, symbolic manner. Emblem books, like *Stammbücher,* were heavily dependent on proverb collections. [45] Schöne's argument that the emblem books had a direct effect on the language of Baroque tragedy strengthens the assumption that in all areas of seventeenth-century literature there was a tendency to think epigrammatically, that is, in single poetic examples. The popularity and influence of all these poetic small forms contributed to the accumulation of knowledge and wisdom by accretion rather than by integration.

The popularity of macaronic epigrams offers another example of the difficulty of extricating what is "native" from what is foreign and the futility of separating *Volkslyrik* from *Kunstlyrik.* It is fair to assume that as long as Latin was a living, vigorous language spoken in school and university, anyone who knew how to read and write, and a good many illiterates as well, knew a few Latin words and phrases well and could recognize and understand a few more. As in any bilingual situation, the humorous possibilities of macaronic verse were widely appreciated. As a book inscription we find:

> Hic liber est mein,
> Ideo nomen scripsi drein.
> Si vis hunc librum stehlen,
> Pendebis an der kehlen.
> Tunc veniunt die raben
> Et volunt tibi oculos ausgraben.

---

[44] Albrecht Schöne, *Emblematik und Drama im Zeitalter des Barock* (Munich, 1964), p. 21.

[45] Ibid., pp. 56-57.

Tunc clamabis ach, ach, ach,
Ubique tibi recte geschach. [46]

A house inscription reads:

Wer will bauen an der Strassen,
Muss die Leute reden lassen.

But it also occurs with this variation:

Qui vult aedificare an der Strassen,
Debet stultum dicere lassen;
Optat mihi quisque was er will
Opto ei noch so viel. [47]

In both these verses Latin, as the learned language, has the effect of parodied wisdom, while the familiar German is down-to-earth and anticlimatic. The humor depends on the balance between the two, a balance slightly in favor of the vernacular because the rhyme words are in German. The repeated shift from one language to the other in every line produces a jar that parodies the caesura of the alexandrine. In the last verse quoted, this jolt is increased by the extra Latin syllables in lines 1 and 3. The great dependency of the verse on all these elements can be demonstrated by translating it back into German and smoothing out the rhythm:

Wer will bauen an der Strassen,
Muss den Dummen reden lassen;
Wünsch mir jeder was er will,
Wünsch ich ihm genau so viel.

Now the poem is uninteresting because it no longer looks like a cracked plate.

Another humorous possibility of the macaronic poem is incorrect or interpretative translation. The device is perhaps most familiar as it is used in Schiller's *Wallensteins Lager,* in the "Kapuziner-

---

[46] Wilhelm Wattenbach, *Das Schriftwesen im Mittelalter* (Leipzig, 1896), p. 534.

[47] Forck, *Deutsche Inschriften,* p. 15. Forck modernizes spelling and punctuation.

predigt," where he copied it effectively from Abraham a Santa Clara. For example:

> Ubi erit victoriae spes,
> Si offenditur Deus? Wie soll man siegen,
> Wenn man die Predigt schwänzt und die Mess,
> Nichts tut als in den Wirtshäusern liegen?

and:

> Was sagt der Prediger? Contenti estote,
> Begnügt euch mit eurem Kommissbrote.

Interpretative translation shows a sheer joy in language, a delight in its possibilities — its potential to confuse as well as to enlighten. It could be used to mislead or to seduce, as in the following *Stammbuchvers* with its Mephistophelean mixture of learning and lewdness:

> Sis felix,
>   Gehe fleisig zu Frauen-Zimmer,
> Sis potens,
>   Halte dich fein wohl bey ihnen,
> Et Deus te servet,
>   Gott gebe Glück und Seegen darzu,
> Studiosa Corona,
>   Dass ein wackerer Student daraus werde. [48]
>
>   (1685)

Sometimes a few Latin words greatly expand the expressiveness of the German, as in this poem by Logau:

>   werben
>   Cogere milites, Soldaten
>   zwingen
>   Mars verhönt nur das Latein,
>   Muss doch selbst Lateinisch seyn.
>   Wil er Wölcker an sich bringen,
>   Muss er vor die Knechte zwingen.   (vor = zuvor)
>
>   (I, 1, 64)

---

[48] Keil and Keil, *Deutsche Stammbücher,* p. 109.

But macaronic verses were not always humorous. Epitaphs sometimes appeared in both a Latin and a German version. Some of these are handled with so much skill and imagination as to refute the trite and well-worn assertion that the Latin model stifled the German creative impulse. In the following example from 1568 the German adaptation, though inspired by the Latin, is not merely a translation but a different poem:

> Hic iacet in tumba Rosa mundi, non Rosamunda:
> Non redolet, set olet, quae redolere solet.

> Ein Ros allhie begraben leit
> Von schön berümpt sehr weit und breit;
> Jetzt ist es nur ein madensack,
> Den niemand sehn noch riechen mag. [49]

Because the Latin puns are untranslatable, the German poet did not attempt a translation. But he independently added the image of the "madensack" and used a popular meter to render the Latin distich, producing a poem that one would not suspect of having a Latin source.

Latin and German, epigram and proverb, learning and popular wisdom — the writers of the age did not keep them apart but freely used the one to reenforce the other. This reenforcement is demonstrated vividly in Grimmelshausen's *Bartkrieg,* [50] a story in which an argument arises over the merits and shortcomings of red beards. Three views from three authorities are quoted, all of them in epigrammatic form. The first, an old wives' notion (*die alten Mütterlein*), reads:

> Die Rotbärt sollst du nicht schelten,
> Die Schwarzbärt geraten selten.

From this popular verse Grimmelshausen takes a leap to the classics, and to none other than Martial, the epigrammatist *par excellence,* whose opinion in the matter of beards, the narrator claims,

---

[49] Quoted by Seiler, *Sprichwörterkunde,* p. 127, after Bruno Seidel, *Sententiae proverbiales de moribus* ... (Basel, 1568).

[50] Johann von Grimmelshausen, *Simplicianische Schriften,* ed. Alfred Kelletat (Darmstadt, 1965), pp. 689-707.

has become proverbial: "dessen Meinung allbereits ... zu einem gemeinen Sprichwort worden." The text is quoted in Latin:

> Crine ruber, niger ore, brevis pede, lumine laesus,
> Rem magnam praestas Zoile, si bonus es. [51]

To substantiate his claim of popularity for Martial, Grimmelshausen translates the Latin into a clumsy but effectively unacademic *Knittelvers*:

> Rothaar, Schwarzmaul, Stollfuss, Scheelaug,
> Gross Wunder ists, wenn solcher taug.

The third verse is called *altfränkisch,* and its author is respectfully described as "der kunstreiche uralte Reimenschmied":

> Rote Bärt und Erlenbogen,
> Geraten sie, so soll mans loben.

Of course the whole argument is humorous, but it illustrates nonetheless that the epigram, when it became widely known, had some characteristics of the proverb, and that the proverb, particularly when rhymed and pointed, was nothing but the epigram of the marketplace. Similarly, German and Latin, the languages of home and school respectively, often met in the small forms where no pedantry kept them apart.

All these verses were *Sprüche.* The epigram was an elegant and literary kind of *Spruch,* which was, however, at any time prone to stoop to the popular level. Classical and indigenous elements, far from mutually excluding one another or forming separate genres, both contributed to the development of the epigram in seventeenth-century Germany. At this point the distinctions between *Volkslyrik* and *Kunstlyrik* become meaningless, even harmful, for they obscure organic relations and interactions which the age itself took for granted.

---

[51] Martial 12. 54.

CHAPTER II

EPITAPHS AND OTHER INSCRIPTIONS

ACTUAL INSCRIPTIONS, THE PRACTICAL SIDE OF THE GENRE, turn it into something of a commodity, into *Gebrauchslyrik*. Which inscriptions belong within the scope of a literary investigation? Clearly not all of them are poems, not even all that employ rhythmic language or rhyme. Is the oldest line of Germanic verse, the alliterative inscription on the Horn of Gallehus, an epigram? If it is, then it provides further proof of an indigenous tradition that developed independently of classical influences and yet belongs to the same farflung family as the inscriptions on Greek sacrificial objects, the so-called dedicatory epigrams of the *Anthology*.

In the sixteenth century the writing of inscriptions on household utensils was not beneath the skill of a Hans Sachs, [1] and the German Humanists collected the inscriptions on the buildings of their cities. [2]

To qualify as a poem, however, an inscription should not only identify an object, in rhythmic language but must in some way transcend the immediate object. The following is an example of a fairly complex inscription that has no poetic merit even though it contains a good deal of information, is written in the form of a poem, and has the distinction of having been composed by Kepler. It appears on a standard measuring vessel (*Normaleimer*) in the Gewerbe-Museum in Ulm:

---

[1] Adelbert von Keller and Edmund Heinrich Goetze, eds., *Hans Sachs,* Bibliothek des Litterarischen Vereins in Stuttgart, vol. 207 (Tubingen, 1895), 23: 316-17, 434, 474-76, 484-85.

[2] Fritz Viktor Arens, ed., *Die Inschriften der Stadt Mainz von frühmittelalterlicher Zeit bis 1650,* Die deutschen Inschriften, vol. 2 (Stuttgart, 1948), pp. 17-18. Arens mentions a number of sixteenth-century collections.

Zween Schuh mein Tief
Ein Ellen mein Quer,
Ein geeichter Eimer macht mich leer,
Dann sein mir vierthalb Centner blieben,
Voll Donauwasser wieg ich sieben,
Doch lieber mich mit Korne eich,
Und vierundsechzigmal abstreich,
So bist du 90 Imi reich. [3]

A certain historical quaintness may appeal to us, but this should not be confused with esthetic appeal. The verse has no bearing on anything other than the object on which it is written; the device of personification is quite mechanical, and the rhyme is merely a mnemonic device.

It is the execution that limits Kepler's verse. The subject itself, that is, the importance of standard weights and measures, could have been treated within a wider context and thus acquired greater significance, as in an inscription on a glass window, dated 1620, now at the Kunstgewerbe Museum in Berlin:

Hetend wir alle einen gloubenn
Gott und den gemeinen nutz vor ougen
Gut fründ und recht gericht,
Ein Elle mass und gewicht,
Ein müntz und gut gält
So stünd es besser in der wällt. [4]

This poem deplores a disorderly world that lacks a common measure as it lacks a common faith. There is nothing to which all men can adhere, neither in spiritual matters ("gloubenn"), nor in matters of public and private trust ("Gut fründ und recht gericht"), [5] nor in

---

[3] Anton Dreselly, *Grabschriften, Marterl-, Bildstöckl- und Totenbrett-Verse, dann Hausinschriften, Wohn- und Trinkstuben-Reime, Geräthe-Inschriften und andere* (Salzburg, 1900), no. 1247. Dreselly modernized spelling and punctuation. Subsequent references are to Dreselly and epigram number.

[4] Hans Draheim, *Deutsche Reime. Inschriften des 15. Jahrhunderts und der folgenden* (Berlin, 1883), p. 108. Draheim was apparently unaware of the fact that this verse can also be found among Agricola's proverbs (no. 272). This is another example of the interchangeability of proverb and epigram.

[5] Instead of "gut fründ" Agricola wrote "gutten friden." This blends in somewhat better with the other items, which are all matters of public concern.

the matter of inches and pounds. It is typical of the epigrammatic
method that the plight of the world is entirely objectified in a series
of specific complaints. Unlike the inscription on the *Normaleimer,*
this is a poem worth reading for its own sake.

If an inscription appears on an object that is in itself esthetic
and in harmony with its surroundings, its literary qualities will
actually be enhanced within that context. For example, a very beauti-
ful engraved glass goblet, executed in 1680 by Hermann Schwinger
of Nuremberg, shows two men carrying a burden through a cold
and lonely landscape. [6] The inscription reads:

> Deine Last ist meine Last.
> Ruhest du so hab ich Rast.

The verse itself is rather trite, but the finely wrought detail of the
goblet gives it a specific application. Conversely, the inscription
gives meaning to the object, but without the object it is no more
than a generalized pious sentiment.

Epigrammatic art consists largely in striking a fine balance between describing one object or situation and making a statement
that is applicable to other objects or situations. The inscription, in
particular, cannot abandon its descriptive function, but it can be
esthetically pleasing without going far beyond that function. Consider the inscription on the church bell at Mergentheim, dating
from 1594:

> St. Johannes bin ich genannt,
> Durch das Feuer bin ich geflossen,
> J. Arnold von Fulda hat mich gegossen.
> (Dreselly, no. 1166)

This verse is mainly informative, giving the name of the bell and the
name of its maker, and yet it has a genuine literary appeal.
The source of its poetic quality lies in the second line, as one can
clearly see if that line is omitted: "St. Johannes bin ich genannt,/
J. Arnold von Fulda hat mich gegossen." The information and the
continuity have been preserved, but the charm has disappeared.
This second line, "Durch das Feuer bin ich geflossen," contains a

---

[6] Now at the Cleveland Museum of Art, catalog no. 50.389.

reference to the process by which the bell was made and also the rhyme word. The technical allusion must be seen in conjunction with the fact that the bell is not entirely inanimate: it has a voice and a name. "Für den mittelalterlichen Menschen waren Glocken beseelte Wesen und konnten reden." [7] Hence the vivid image, "Durch das Feuer bin ich geflossen," implies, "I have been tested by fire; you can trust me." Boxed in between the lines providing essential information about a specific thing, there is a transcending image of an ordeal by fire. It radiates into the human sphere, implying a kinship between man the maker and the manmade object; the kinship is cemented by the rhyme that flows from the bell to its maker, J. Arnold von Fulda. The bell takes its place in the order of things and creatures that may undergo such a test by fire. The first and third lines establish its uniqueness, but with the second line it acquires significance. In this combination lies the essence of epigrammatic art. Such verses are examples of true epigrams derived from primitive inscriptions.

Bell inscriptions can be found in Latin, in High German, and in Low German. Without exception they employ the first person singular, endowing the bell with a "voice" and almost a personality. A magic quality commonly ascribed to bells is an ability to control the weather:

> Hilf Maria vnd dein liebes Kind
> Das ich vertrib mit meinem Schal
> Die schädlichen Wetter Regen Wind
> Uf Bergen vnd im Tal.

> An dem Tüfel will ich mich rechen
> Mit der Hilf Gottes alle Wetter zerbrechen. [8]

The peculiar attraction of bell inscriptions arises from this belief in their magic potential, delivered in a tone of resounding faith. Schiller must have sensed something of this magic when he chose the bell as a cohesive symbol for one of his longest poems. The epigraph to the poem is the inscription on the big bell in the dome

---

[7] Ernst Schubert, ed., *Die Inschriften der Stadt Naumburg an der Saale. Die deutschen Inschriften*, vol. 7 (Stuttgart, 1960), p. 92.

[8] Draheim, *Deutsche Reime*, p. 2.

of Schaffhausen: "Vivos voco/ mortuos plango/ fulgura frango." [9]
He did justice to the first two lines of the inscription calling on the
living and mourning for the dead but the meaning of the last line
escaped him: he saw the bell as a lifeless object with no power to
break bolts of lightning. Because Schiller's bell is not endowed with
life and with magic powers, the "Lied von der Glocke" is ultimately
not cohesive and the symbol fails. His elaborate technical descriptions of bell making do not connect human lives as they are meant
to do, while the actual bell inscriptions quite naively succeed.

The pattern for bell inscriptions was fairly well set, and they
did not vary much from the fifteenth to the seventeenth century.
House inscriptions, on the other hand, were capable of a great deal
of variation and refinement. Perhaps the most common type is a
simple blessing, such as this one, dated 1608, from a house in
Constance:

> Zum Schafhirten heißt man dies Hauß
> Das behüte der gute Hirt überaus
> Und alle, die gehn ein und aus. [10]

Against this verse we set another blessing that occurs in Innsbruck
in 1647, forty years later, and has distinctly Baroque qualities:

> Dem Haus, das stets in Kriegsgefahr
> Der Sitz Maria's von Ettal war,
> Sei im Frieden nun ein Schild,
> Maria in dem Gnadenbild.
>
> (Dreselly, no. 775)

The structure is bipartite: the first two lines belong to the house
and its owner Maria, the last two to the other, the heavenly, Mary.
The connection is established through the unusual syntax, which
puts the invocation at the end and the dative object with its modify-
ing clause at the beginning. The poem starts with the house in war-
time and moves upward toward peace and the mother of God,
leaving an overall impression of harmony expressive of serene faith.

---

[9] Ibid., p. 3.
[10] Forck, *Deutsche Inschriften*, p. 6.

Among the most popular Baroque house inscriptions are those
that deal with the paradox of owning what one must lose through
death. "Dies Haus ist mein und doch nicht mein" is a common
theme for this type of inscription. [11] The house of the living appears
as an antechamber to the grave; its inscription is similar to an
epitaph. This is not surprising since epitaphs were among the most
fashionable verses of the period.

In seventeenth-century Germany the epitaph occupied for a short
time a very prominent place. It became a literary genre in the sense
that it was written not for use on tombstones but for literary en-
joyment, and not only in isolated instances but in series. No doubt
this preoccupation was part of the Baroque obsession with the
themes of death and decay in general. "Du gehst in dem du gehst
und stehst und ruhst zum Tod," wrote Gryphius in his "Grabschrifft
die er ihm selbst in tötlicher Leibes Schwachheit auffgesetzet," an
epitaph for himself. [12] The epitaph is the most compact expression
of the all-pervading Baroque theme of *Vergänglichkeit*: from Opitz
to Hofmannswaldau to Wernicke, *poetische Grabschrifften* can be
found in abundance in the work of many poets.

While most literary epitaphs were not meant for use on tombstones, it would be a mistake to think of them as entirely divorced
from the cemetery. Many tombstones are embellished with the verses
of contemporary poets, and many anonymous cemetery verses show
the same tendencies that can be observed in the printed epitaph. [13]
It may therefore be assumed that those who composed epitaphs for
tombstones, frequently parsons, were subject to contemporary
standards of taste, and that even when an epitaph was not originally
written for a tombstone, it was often considered suitable. Again
there is a noticeable absence of clear-cut lines between *Volkslyrik*
and *Kunstlyrik*.

The typical Baroque epitaph highlights some detail of human
existence or decay in such a way as to create a state of tension
between the humble, worldly fact described and the ineffable vision

[11] For several examples of verses starting with this line, see ibid., p. 8.
[12] Andreas Gryphius, *Gesamtausgabe der deutschsprachigen Werke*, vol. 2,
Oden und Epigramme, ed. Marian Szyrocki (Tubingen, 1964), p. 201 (hereafter cited as *Oden und Epigramme*).
[13] Dreselly, *Grabschriften*, p. 7.

of death that looms behind the fact. For example, a somewhat pathetic inscription:

> Hier liegt Frau Anna Reiter
> Geborene Sauter von Gmunden;
> Sie sammelte Wurzeln und Kräuter,
> Doch für den Tod hat sie keines gefunden.
>
> (Dreselly, no. 446)

Here the proverbial saying that there is no herb against death is applied to the occupation of the deceased. The image of actual herb gathering, in contrast to the wider significance of the proverb, throws into sharp relief the humdrum of daily existence, the trivia that make up a life. The first three lines identify the dead woman by name, birthplace, and occupation; in the last line her specific occupation merges with the general human condition as she shares the common helplessness of all men in the face of death.

Another inscription reads: "Hier fiel Hans Hasenkopf vom Hausdach in die Ewigkeit." [14] A man with a slightly comical name succumbs to the law of gravity; the cause is trivial, but the effect is transcendent. An identity dissolves in one grotesque moment as Hans Hasenkopf takes an incongruous spill from his rooftop into eternity. "Eben das Zusammenbiegen des Nichtzusammengehörigen scheint der grauenvollen Verwicklung von Leben und Tod einigermassen zu entsprechen," writes Robert Petsch with regard to popular cemetery inscriptions. [15] In his book *Spruchdichtung des Volkes* Petsch confines himself to actual gravestones and thus he does not see the fashionable literary movement that encouraged the grotesque epitaph. Written in 1938, the book is imbued with admiration of whatever could be considered *volkstümlich*. One must beware of the tendency in some German studies to praise grotesque humor in a popular context and to censure the very same quality in well-known poets as "decadent," for during the seventeenth century a satirical attitude toward death and the dead can be found on various levels of literacy.

Many literary epitaphs are occupational. Indebted to the medieval tradition of the dance of death, they show men cut off while

---

[14] Petsch, *Spruchdichtung,* p. 128.
[15] Ibid., p. 131.

exercising their various trades. The most common variant is like Frau Anna Reiter's epitaph: man's skill in making a living will not keep him from dying. The merit of these poems is directly dependent on the effectivness of specific details of the deceased person's craft, as a comparison of epitaphs will illustrate. The first is Opitz's "Grabschrifft eines Schmiedes":

> Ihr Freunde, glaubet allzumahl,
> Könnt Eisen, Fewer, Flamm, und Stahl
> Deß grimmen Todes macht obsiegen,
> Ich wolte wohl jetzt hier nit liegen. [16]

Opitz goes no further than to mention the basic materials of the smith's profession, fire and metal; the reference is vague because the actual processes of the smith's craft are omitted. The poem is further weakened by repetition or near repetition: iron, steel; flame, fire. The next example, Logau's "Grabschrifft eines Schusters," is considerably more accomplished:

> Künte man das Leben strecken, wie man kan das Leder dehnen,
> Hätt ich, das ich hier nicht läge, trauen künnen meinen Zähnen.

> (ZD 117)

This epitaph, one of Logau's late verses, shows him in perfect command of the technique of the epigram. [17] The shoemaker's life and his trade are identified by a precise and humorous image. Taking the image one logical step further, the poet compares man's tenacious clinging to life to the shoemaker's pulling the leather with his teeth. He makes the most of the fact that "Leben" and "Leder" alliterate: the first line is made up of two perfectly parallel halves divided by a strict caesura, and the two substantives occupy identical positions in the rhythmic structure of their respective half-lines. A wistful subjunctive is used for the shoemaker's impossible desires.

---

[16] Martin Opitz, *Teutsche Poemata,* ed. Georg Witkowski, Neudrucke deutscher Litteraturwerke, nos. 189-92 (Halle, 1902), p. 136 (no. 125). Subsequent references are to Witkowski and epigram number.

[17] Logau's editor, Gustav Eitner, has shown that Logau published his epigrams in chronological order of composition. See Eitner, *Friedrichs von Logau Sämtliche Sinngedichte,* pp. 739-42.

Under the aspect of eternity all occupations seem futile. Opitz describes the bellows maker who lacks wind, that is, breath, in "Grabschrifft eines Blassbalckmachers":

> O Lieber Mensch, dein Leben ja betrachte,
> Hier liget, der die Blassebälge machte,
> Jetzt aber nun zuletzt es doch sich findt,
> Dem Meister, Schau, gebrist noch selber Windt.
>
> (Witkowski, no. 122)

In "Grabschrifft eines fahrenden Bothen" Wernicke shows the professional messenger who has no carriage for his return:

> Der halb in Hamburg wohnt' und halb in Kopenhagen,
> Und Leute, Pack, und Brief' in ein Register schrieb:
> Und offt an einen Orth, doch nirgends lange blieb:
> Der läg auch nicht so lang' in dieser Herberg' hier.
> Wär hier ein Wagen nur der auch zurücke führ.
>
> (VIII, 26)

Logau, who wrote occupational epitaphs throughout his career, describes the weaver and the tailor in "Grabmal eines Webers" and "Grabschrifft eines Schneiders":

> Ein Weber liegt allhier; sein Faden ist zerrissen,
> Weiss keinen Weber-Knopff, denselben auszubüssen.
>
> (I, 10, 33)

> Hier liegt ein Schneider in der Ruh,
> Der manche Löcher flickte zu.
> Ietzt kan er ihm die Haut nicht flicken, (ihm = sich)
> Die ihm die Würmer ganz zerstücken.
>
> (I, 3, 59)

The latter epitaph contains a grotesque image that fascinated Renaissance and Baroque poets alike: the image of man, the highest creature, eaten by what was considered the lowest, the worm. This idea, sharpened into the image of the eater who is eaten, is best known in the words of Hamlet who, when asked for the whereabouts of Polonius, replies that he is at supper: "Not where he eats, but where he is eaten; a certain convocation of politic worms are e'en now at him" (act 4, scene 3). In German the theme of the cook eaten by worms can be found in many versions (including two poems by Logau, I, 1, 14 and ZD 124), but perhaps the best is "Grabschrifft eines Kochs" by Opitz, who adds the final touch of ignominy — he who cooked food is eaten unceremoniously and raw:

> Wie wird die Welt doch vberall verkehret,
> Hie hat ein Koch im grabe seine ruh,
> Der mancherley von Speissen richtet zu,
> Jetzt haben ihn die Würme roh verzehret.
>   (Witkowski, no. 121)

Sometimes death assumes the occupation of his victim and appears to him, as it were, in the victim's own guise. In the somewhat too elaborate description of "Grabschrifft eines Jägers" Opitz shows us the hunted hunter:

> In dieser holen Klufft gesuchet hat sein läger,
> Ein grausamer Tyrann und Fein der Wilden thier,
> Jetzt hat er wiederumb auch seinen Lohn darfür,
> Der Todt der war sein Hundt, die Kranckheit war sein Jäger,
> So ist der Jäger nun, wie kühn er sey und starck,
> Gejaget durch den Todt hier under disen Sarck.
>   (Witkowski, no. 123)

Again in "Grabschrifft eines Fischers," Logau follows the master's lead but improves on him in compactness of image, economy of words, and macabre detail:

> Hier fischt ein Fischer ietzt im Sande, der vor im
>   Wasser hat gefischt;
> Der Tod hat ihn, wie er die Fische, nunmehr in seinem
>   Garn erwischt.
>   (ZD 118)

This kind of epitaph parodies the idea of divine justice: death treats man as man treats the animals and fish. But one step further, and even the parody dissolves in the absurdity of death, as when the musician becomes the musical instrument in "Grabschrifft eines höltzernen Musicanten":

> Ich habe mit dem Hackebret viel Lebenszeit vertrieben;
> Ietzt klappert nun der schlimme Kerl, der Tod, mit
>   meinen Rieben.   (Rieben = Rippen)
>   (ZD 113)

In such images as "der schlimme Kerl, der Tod," the treatment of death has become secularized and almost lighthearted: death is the ungracious intruder in the festivities or the business of life. [18] This attitude, too, can be found in cemeteries as well as in books. In the following inscription from a tombstone, which is contemporary with Logau's *Sinngedichte,* death appears as an unwelcome customer:

> Hier liegt begraben Christoph Katzenberger,
> Im Leben gewester Buchdrucker, welchem der Tod
> Anno 1653 den 3. Junii umb 4 Uhr in der Frühe,
> Ein unverhofftes Decret gebracht, ohne Press,
> Schrift, Farb, Papier abzutrucken.
>
> (Dreselly, no. 159)

Parodying the contrast between flesh and soul, the traditional theme of epitaph and funeral oration, Logau writes his "Grabschrifft eines Fleischers":

> Weil ich lebte, kunt ich Beine wol so hoch als Fleisch
> verkauffen;
> Würmen schenck ich ietzt was fleischicht; Beine bleiben
> überm Hauffen.
>
> (ZD 112)

Logau twists the image so that the opposite of flesh, or rather of meat, is not soul or spirit but bones; the thoughts of the butcher continue in death on the level to which they were accustomed in life. Gryphius sums up the contrast between work and death in the starkest epitaph of this type, "Grabschrifft eines gehenckten Seilers":

> Was disen Leib erhält/ muss offt den Leib verderben.
> Ich lebte von dem Strick und muss durch Stricke sterben.
>
> (II, 45)

The Baroque tendency to treat every subject under its crassest, most extreme aspect is startlingly manifested in the lascivious epitaph. To be sure, the mingling of the themes of love and death

---

[18] A remarkably similar phrase occurs in Shakespeare's Sonnet 32: "When that churl Death my bones with dust shall cover." One is led to wonder whether the cognates "churl" and "Kerl" had identical meanings in the seventeenth century.

was nothing new, and earlier poets had painted the decay of beauty in vivid colors, as in the following passage from *Der Ackermann und der Tod*:

Benim und zeuch ab der schönsten frauen des sneiders farbe, so sihestu ein schemliche tocken, ein schiere swelkende blumen von kurze taurendem scheine und einen balde faulenden erdenknollen.

(chap. 24)

But the Baroque treatment differs in its violent blending of sexual details with details of decay, apparently intending to shock the reader into a greater awareness of the immanence of death. I quote from several poets to show the prevalence of this type of epitaph.

Grabschrifft eines geilen Weibs (Opitz)
Hier lieget ein sehr schön, doch geiles Weib begraben,
Wünscht ihr nicht, dass sie ruh soll in der Erden haben,
Sie hat dem Himmel gleich zu werden sich geübt,
Vnd nichts als stetige bewegung mehr gelibt.

(Witkowski, no. 127)

Grabschrifft einer Hure (Logau)
Hier liegt, die gerne lag;
Hat immer Nacht für Tag,
Weil als der Tag die Nacht
Ihr mehr Belieben bracht.
Nur diss ist ihr Beschwer:
Die Armen sind ihr leer.
Der Tod liegt ihr am Arm
Und macht ihr doch nicht warm;
Die so geliebte Schoss
Deckt jetzt ein Erdenkloss.

(II, 2, 46)

Grabschrifft einer Wittib (Hofmannswaldau)
Ich war ein schönes Schiff, das ohne Ladung lag/
Es plagte mich die Nacht/ es kränkte mich der Tag.
Hier ist nicht Licht genung/ mich deutlich zu verstehen/
Weil mir der Mast gebrach/ muss ich zu Grunde gehen. [19]

---

[19] Hofmann von Hofmannswaldau, *Geistliche Oden, vermischte Gedichte und poetische Grabschrifften* (Breslau, 1696), p. 84.

On the other hand, we also find the opposite paradox, *galante Grabschriften*. "Grabschrifft auff den leichen-stein einer freundin" by Hofmannswaldau has all the mannered exaggerations of the typical complimentary poem of the age, with the difference that it purports to be engraved on a tombstone:

> Ein stern der tugenden/ die sonne dieser stadt/
> Ein engel/ wenn man will den nahmen recht erwegen/
>   Ein licht/ so in der welt mit lust geschienen hat/
> Muss sich dem tode nun zu seinen füssen legen.
>   Mein leser/ liss doch recht/ was ich dir kund getahn;
> Ich habe viel gesagt/ noch aber mehr verschwiegen;
>   Wo hier stern/ sonne/ licht und engel wohnen kan/
> So muss der himmel ja in diesem grabe liegen. [20]

The tone is purposefully inappropriate in its attempted fusion of chivalry and death. The last line in particular fully exploits the setting for this piece of misplaced gallantry. As in the majority of epitaphs that have been cited, the stress is on the irreconcilability of life and death — hence the jarring images and the often shocking combinations. A later age turned in distaste from all these epitaphs, seeing in them only the absence of conventional piety toward the dead and an unfeeling callousness. In fact, the taste for epitaphs died away while the epigram itself was still very much in vogue. Lessing and Ramler did not include any epitaphs in their selective edition of Logau's works; [21] presumably the new culture of *Empfindsamkeit* had no place for wit on the gravestone. However, the Baroque poet's undeniable callousness is deliberate and significant. Surely all this fanciful and highly sophisticated humor constitutes an attempt to stave off the terror of death. In its own way it conveys the same defiance that the folk song expresses in the words: "Trutz Tod, komm her, ich fürcht dich nit!"

But the clash of irreconcilables does not always give off a spark of humor. Gryphius, who lacked a sense of humor despite his

---

[20] Benjamin Neukirch, *Benjamin Neukirchs Anthologie ... erster theil*, ed. Angelo George de Capua and Ernst Alfred Philippson, Neudrucke deutscher Literaturwerke, new ser., vol. 1 (Tubingen, 1961), p. 49.

[21] Walter Heuschkel, *Untersuchungen über Ramlers und Lessings Bearbeitung von Sinngedichten Logaus* (diss., Jena, 1901), p. 5. Heuschkel stated the fact but gave no reason for the conspicuous omission.

comedies, produced few epitaphs, but they are among the most poignant of the age. The structure he usually employed is taut antithesis, as in the following pair:

> Grabschrifft eines Seligen
> Mein Leben war nur Angst/ itzt leb ich stets bey Gott.
> For Lust/ itzt Schmertzen frey. Ist dann mein Tod ein Tod? (For=früher)
>
> (I, 57)

> Grabschrifft eines Verdammten
> Ich lebt in kurtzer Lust/ nun quält mich stete Noht.
> Mein ewig-sterben lebt. Ist dann mein Tod ein Tod?
>
> (I, 58)

The contrasts are placed one within the other, Chinese-box fashion; the two contrasting epitaphs, each ending with the same question, have an overall framework. One would expect complementary answers, yes in the first poem, no in the second. Yet the implied answers are also identical: death is not death from the vantage point of either heaven or hell. The implied meanings of these implied identical answers are salvation and damnation respectively. The reader must supply the final antithesis himself. In addition, each of the two epitaphs contains its own contrast, the focal point being the heavy accent before the caesura of the first line. The key word in this position is "Angst" for the blessed, "Lust" for the damned. For the blessed, earthly life was a terror and true life begins only with the afterlife. For the damned, the argument is reversed and dying is only the beginning of a never-ending process of death. In the same way "Gott" and "Noht" occupy identical positions, but "Gott" contrasts with "Angst," "Noht" with "Lust." Opposites meet and pull apart; heaven and hell open up for a moment and touch briefly, as on a Baroque stage. The same skill and technique can be observed in "Grabschrifft Basiliae," where a triple contrast is boxed within two lines:

> Traurt nicht um meinen Todt/ nicht ich/ ihr könnt verderben/
> Was unterging/ geht auff/ ich leb ihr werdet sterben.
>
> (III, 56)

The thought is deeply traditional and can be found on innumerable graves. What is peculiar to Gryphius is the series of contrasting pairs: "nicht ich / ihr," "unterging / geht auff," and, summing up the two others, "ich leb ihr werdet sterben."

This concern with extraordinary stylistic effects is matched by a preference for extraordinary subject matter. As Assmann von Abschatz wrote love poems to deformed women, epitaph writers were fascinated with unusual deaths. The first example is again from Logau, who is often praised for his supposed healthy straightforwardness — a reputation he acquired because of an unrepresentative selection in modern anthologies. Actually he fully shared the taste of his time for the sensational, as is evident in "Grabschrifft einer schwangern Frauen":

> Hier liegt ein Grab im Grab, und in dess Grabes Grabe,
> Was Welt noch nie gesehn, ihm auch nicht Namen gabe;
> Das Grab begrub zuvor, eh Grab begraben war;
> Zwei Gräber sind nur Eins, und eine Leich ein Paar.
>
> (II, 8, 33)

Here the death of a mother and her unborn child has been intellectualized into a word-and-number game. The exclusion of sentiment, the obsessive stress on the objective facts, permits the poet to concentrate on the precariousness of a life that is dependent on another life as mortal as its own.

It was Gryphius who carried this arithmetical game furthest in "Grabschrifft Laeliae, welcher sich selbst erschossen," an epitaph that is virtually unknown yet has a peculiar and unique greatness:

> Hir ligt in einer Grufft/ der Kläger/ der beklagte/
> Der Recht sprach/ der gezeugt/ und der die Zeugen fragte/
> Und der das Recht aussführt/ und der so must erbleichen:
> Du zehlest siben zwar und findst nur eine Leichen.
>
> (III, 86)

Gryphius's image of a suicide is a court of law in which a man accuses himself and bears witness against himself, cross-examines and judges himself, and finally executes himself: thus, the image of a man who is seven times divided and at odds with himself. The poet condenses this state of mind into three lines, and in the fourth he sums up the paradox of self-hatred and self-destruction in terms of a mathematical puzzle. With the detachment of a court recorder he recounts the sevenfold turmoil that ended with the death of one desperate man.

Probably the only epitaph of the period which is nowadays fairly well known and can be found in many modern anthologies is Gryphius's "Grabschifft Marianae Gryphiae seines Bruders Pauli Töchterlein" (III, 50), a poem of eight lines that is indeed unequaled for compact expression of violence and terror:

> Gebohren in der Flucht/ umbringt mit Schwerd und Brand/
> Schir in dem Rauch erstückt/ der Mutter herbes Pfand/
> Des Vatern höchste Frucht/ die an das Licht gedrungen/
> Als die ergrimmte Glutt mein Vaterland verschlungen.
> Ich habe dise Welt beschawt und bald gesegnet:
> Weil mir auff einen Tag all Angst der Welt begegnet.
> Wo ihr die Tage zehlt; so bin ich jung verschwunden/
> Sehr alt; wofern ihr schätzt/ was ich für Angst empfunden. [22]

Although the four couplets are not divided into stanzas, the poem clearly has two parts. A natural pause occurs after the fourth line where modern usage would set a colon; there the long introductory clause ends and the main sentence begins. The fifth line opens with an "ich" that is almost unexpected, for until then the reader has not been allowed to realize that the speaker is also the victim of the calamities described in the first four lines. (The "mein" in line 4 gives a hint, but it could also refer to the poet.) The first part shows the violence into which the child is born; the second, the terror she experiences. The first concentrates on her surroundings; the second, on her feelings. Each part repeats the contrast in metaphorical terms. Lines three and four give us "Licht," the daylight into which the girl is born, and "die ergrimmte Glutt," the destructive light of arson. Paradoxically, these two lights are identical, for the daylight of this particular newborn child is a city going up in flames; her world is illuminated by arson. The two lights literally flare together, becoming one image. After the significant "ich" the poem turns inward

---

[22] Compare three much inferior but related sonnets in book II: number 34 ("Auf seines Sohnes Theodori Absterben"), number 42 ("Auf eines Adelichen Frauenzimmers Absterben"), and number 43 ("Auf das Absterben eines Adelichen Kindes an die betrübte Frau Mutter"). Andreas Gryphius, *Gesamtausgabe der deutschsprachigen Werke*, vol. I, *Sonette*, ed. Hugh Powell (Tubingen, 1963), pp. 111, 115, 116.

toward the feelings and, most important, toward the death wish of the baby. The antithesis of the two lights in the first part is parallel to the "jung / alt" antithesis of the last two lines. Objectively, by the count of the world, the child was young; subjectively, by the count in which terror tells time, she was ancient. What is obvious in this poem lies hidden in all the other epitaphs that have been quoted: a terror so extreme that it can be borne only by the exertion of a faith that equals the terror in desperate intensity, or by the assertion of reason. Reason is helpless to do more than play with the facts and concept of death, but precisely by playing with them it is possible for the doomed mortal mind to assert itself, especially with the introduction of humor and its attendant exclusion of pity, including self-pity.

The literary epitaph had a short life. Tastes changed and a later generation shrank from its stark, uncompromising qualities. Toward the end of the seventeenth century, poets favored the historical epitaph celebrating famous villains such as Nero and Messalina. Wernicke wrote a good many of these. Still later the epitaph completely dropped out of epigrammatic practice. But while it lasted, the Baroque epitaph bridged the gap between the worldly and the religious epigram: a single alexandrine often contains both life and the afterlife, separated only by a caesura. Because of its borderline position between two worlds and two kinds of poetry, the Baroque epitaph is in some ways the epigram *par excellence* of the seventeenth century.

Chapter III

THE POLEMICAL EPIGRAM

THE PRECEDING CHAPTERS HAVE STRESSED THE DEPENDENCE OF THE EPIGRAM on other small forms. This chapter will turn the other way and ask: How, where, and when did a poet writing in German first claim to have written epigrams, and what are they? The customary answer to the first question is to give credit to Opitz, whose *Teutsche Poemata* appeared in 1624. However, the anthology that Zincgref appended to this edition of Opitz's poems includes epigrams by other poets. Therefore the form must have been practiced before it received its decisive impetus from Opitz.

However, the first epigrams were written even earlier than those in Zincgref's anthology. At the threshold of German epigrammatic poetry is a sixteenth-century work of much charm and merit entitled *D. Ambrosii Lobwassers Deutsche Zierliche Epigrammata von allen Ständen vnd leuten in gemein.* These epigrams are single stanzas, each one self-contained and hortatory, dealing with the particular temptations to which a given trade or calling is exposed. An example is "Koch vnd Keller," number 106:

> Der Koch vnd Kellr/
> Tügn offt kein Hellr/
> Heimlicher weiss/
> Sie Tranck vnd Speiss/
> Zusammen tragn/
> Der Koch thut sagn:
> Hab dir ein Wurst/
> Lesch mir den Durst/
> Leben offt besser denn der Fürst.

The author, Ambrosius Lobwasser, died in 1585. His epigrams are so unknown that they pose certain bibliographical and historical problems which must be discussed before we can turn to the contents of the little book itself. The difficulty in proving that Lobwasser deserves the claim of priority here made for him lies in the fact that the work can be traced only in seventeenth-century editions. It is therefore possible that a seventeenth-century editor added the fashionable word "epigrams" to the title. As long as we lack the sixteenth-century originals of the seventeenth-century editions, we cannot be certain how and under what heading Lobwasser published them. But there is convincing evidence that Lobwasser was indeed the first to introduce the vernacular epigram to Germany.

Lobwasser is known to both literary and religious historians. Not only the *Allgemeine Deutsche Biographie* but also religious encyclopedias and works on church music contain substantial biographical information about him. He was a widely traveled Saxon jurist; his limited fame rests on his translation of the Huguenot psalter, which he turned into German in such a way that the original melodies could be used with the translated text. His version was so skillful that it lasted well into the eighteenth century; Goethe was familiar with it. [1] Moreover, in his translation of Psalm 89 Lobwasser employed a German alexandrine for the first time, as Erich Trunz has pointed out. Yet the possibility of a French influence on Lobwasser's epigrams has never been mentioned. On the contrary it has been explicitly denied in one of the two comments I found concerning his epigrams. Richard Levy dismissed them with the words: "Die Epigramme des Ambrosius Lobwasser haben mit den Opitzschen nur den Namen gemein und sind nach Form und Inhalt noch durchaus volkstümlich, auch verraten sie keinerlei ausländische Beeinflussung." [2] This is a hasty judgment; Lobwasser's life and work belie such a statement. He was very much open to foreign influences and translated not only Psalms from the French but also hymns of the church fathers from the Latin. Levy simply made the usual fateful assumption that learning and an indigenous content are mutually

---

[1] Erich Trunz, "Die deutschen Übersetzungen des Hugenottenpsalters," *Euphorion* 29 (1928): 578-617. See also p. 15, note 11.

[2] Richard Levy, *Martial und die deutsche Epigrammatik des siebzehnten Jahrhunderts* (Stuttgart, 1903), p. 13.

exclusive. I should like to suggest that a foreign influence, that of Clément Marot, the chief author of the Huguenot psalter, is very likely. Marot is also considered the first epigrammatist in any modern European language. [3] It stands to reason that as his translator and admirer, Lobwasser would have been familiar with his other work as well and would have used it as he saw fit.

There are apparently three editions of Lobwasser's epigrams. The first, dated 1611, was described by Ernst Höpfner in an obscure publication. [4] Apart from Levy, whose cryptic comment has been quoted in its entirety, Höpfner seems to have been the only scholar who studied the book, although he, too, gave it no more than a page of comment. He quoted the following title: "E. D. Ambrosij Lobwassers zierliche nützliche vnd artige Deutsche Epigrammata. Von allerley Ständen vnd Leuten in gemein. Jetzo mit fleiss aus etzlichen Büchern vnd Bibliotheken zusammengebracht vnd vermehret, durch J. A. H. T. Leipzig, Typis Tobiae Beyeri. Gedruckt durch Lorentz Kober, in vorlegung Thomae Schürers, 1611." It should be noted that the editor, "J. A. H. T.," claimed considerable credit for himself.

The second edition for which there is evidence was listed by Goedeke and is dated 1612, without place of publication. [5] Höpfner mentioned Leipzig in his title quote. He conjectured that Goedeke was dealing with the same edition which he himself described and that Goedeke simply made a mistake in the date. [6] But if that was the case, Goedeke must have overlooked the place of publication in addition to mistaking the date. This is unlikely. It is more likely that there were two editions — one of 1611 available to Höpfner and one of 1612 available to Goedeke — and that their rapid succession is simply a sign that the book sold well. Indeed, it must have been

---

[3] For Marot's epigrams see Clément Marot, *Œuvres Complètes* (Paris, 1824), 2: 327-548; for his position among European epigrammatists, see Hutton, *Greek Anthology in France,* p. 301.

[4] Ernst Höpfner, *Reformbestrebungen auf dem Gebiete der deutschen Dichtung des XVI. und XVII. Jahrhunderts,* Jahresbericht des K. Wilhelm-Gymnasium in Berlin (Berlin, 1866), pp. 36-37.

[5] Karl Goedeke, *Grundriss zur Geschichte der deutschen Dichtung,* 2d ed. (Dresden, 1886), 2: 173.

[6] Of course Höpfner, writing in 1866, used an older edition of Goedeke than the one cited in note 5. However, the entry for Lobwasser did not change.

successful since it was still being published in 1634, a fact of which neither Höpfner nor Goedeke was aware.

A copy of the 1634 edition is part of the Konrad Burdach collection now at the library of the University of California at Berkeley. [7] The book is an attractive duodecimo volume measuring 6.2 cm by 12.4 cm. The frontispiece is an engraving of the author; the title page reads:

D. Ambrosii
Lobwassers
Deutsche Zierliche
Epigrammata

von allen Ständen
vnd leuten in gemein

A separate page at the end of the volume states simply: "Gedruckt im Jahr 1634." The volume contains 185 epigrams in a form like that of the example quoted on page 58. The pages and the verses themselves are unnumbered, and the signatures seem to have been tampered with, perhaps by an earlier binder.

Each stanza consists of nine lines, of which the first eight have four syllables each and the last has eight. That Lobwasser counted syllables is indicated by the fact that some words ending on *er* are syncopated, while others are not. Thus: "Die Newe Preistr / Durch New Registr" (no. 18); but: "Die Prediger / Mit reiner Lehr" (no. 20). A correct syllable count was more important to Lobwasser than consistency in spelling or pronunciation. Similarly with *en*: the title of number 12 is "Mönch vond Pfaffen," but the first line is "Die Mönch vond Pfaffn" in the interest of restricting the line to the requisite number of syllables. This principle is operative throughout the volume.

The rhyme scheme of each stanza is *aa, bb, cc, ddd*. The final three-line rhyme and the double length of the last line round off

---

[7] No other copy is listed in any other library catalog, including German ones, as far as I had access to them. Nor does any available bibliography mention the 1634 edition itself. The copy at Berkeley is therefore almost certainly the only copy in the United States. Faber du Faur, *German Baroque Literature: A Catalogue of the Collection of the Yale University Library* (New Haven, Conn., 1958), pp. 9-10, lists nothing but the psalter. In his comments, Faber du Faur followed the article by Trunz very closely.

the stanza and give it the appearance of a self-contained unit. Similar effects can be found in Hans Sach's poetry, but Sachs never wrote a stanza quite like Lobwasser's. Moreover, Sachs used strophes only in longer poems, never singly. His *Sprüche* are rhyming two-line poems of equal length. On the other hand, Marot's *Épigrammes* have a great deal of strophic variety. Although Marot, like Sachs, does not use a stanza precisely the same as Lobwasser's, it seems reasonable to assume that he pointed the way toward greater technical facility and experimentation.

Of the 185 epigrams in Lobwasser's book, 43 are signed "I. A." These were no doubt written by the editor of the 1611 edition who, as Höpfner mentioned, took credit for collecting and expanding the verses. But the book's continuity makes it extremely unlikely that its components were ever dispersed as I. A. claimed they were. Moreover, I. A.'s own verses, while imitating Lobwasser's, tend to break the continuity rather than contribute to it. I. A. attacked general vices rather than those of specific callings as Lobwasser did. Neither in form nor in content did I. A. show any perception or originality that would convince us he organized the book or called it *Epigrammata* thirteen years before the appearance of Opitz's *Teutsche Poemata*. The intrinsic evidence supports the assumption that the poet who first brought the alexandrine from France to Germany was the same poet who first brought the epigram from France to Germany — namely, Lobwasser.

Lobwasser's book is not a haphazard collection of miscellanies as the work of later epigrammatists often was, for Lobwasser took on no less than all of society. He preserved a medieval structure in the arrangement of his verses, although the spirit is resolutely Protestant. He is a curiously transitional figure, standing between Hans Sachs and the French, between Renaissance and Reformation, between the old *Spruch* and the new epigram. He began his book with the clergy, starting with the pope, ending with the village parson. He continued with *weltliche Stände* and then turned to the domestic order ("Von Hausswirtschafft"), where he dealt with desirable and undesirable behavior of husbands, wives, daughters, sons, and engaged couples. This is followed by a final section, "Von Sünd vnd Lastern," largely composed by I. A.

The idea of characterizing the various estates in brief satirical verses was not new, and rhyming these was in the tradition of the

Narrenschiff. Lobwasser's inspiration may have been Hans Sachs, whose *Eygentliche Beschreibung Aller Stände auff Erden,* published in Nuremberg in 1568, was illustrated by Jost Amman — another example of a book that combined pictures and brief verses. [8] Sachs described each vocation in eight lines of *Knittelvers.* These poems are not rounded wholes since any number of lines might have been added without changing the structure of the preceding lines. Moreover, where Lobwasser ended on a criticism, often a sharp one, Sachs was very rarely critical, usually contenting himself with a merely informative description of the trade in question. A comparison will show how truly epigrammatic Lobwasser is:

> Koch (Sachs)
> Ich pin ain koch. Fuer erber gest   (erber = ehrbare)
> Kan ich wol kochen auf das pest
> Reis, pfeffer, ander guet gemües,
> Vogel, fisch, sulzcen, res und sües;
> Für den pauren und hantwercks-mon
> Hirs, gersten, linsen, erbeis, pon,
> Rotseck, wuerst, suppen, ruebn und krawt,
> Darmit sie auch fuellen ir hawt. [9]

> Küchen Meister (Lobwasser)
> Küchenmeistr gut/
> Offt vnterm Hut/
> Spielt mit der Würtz/
> Nach seinem Nutz/
> Entzeugt der Speiss/
> Heimlicher Weiss/
> Gebürligkeit/
> Wird ihm nicht leidt/
> Rath/ woher kompt sein schönes Kleid.

(no. 99)

Sachs's poem is a rhymed description, but Lobwasser's is a polemical epigram.

The section on the clergy is virulently belligerent. The hierarchical arrangement of the epigrams implies that Lobwasser believed in a rigidly structured and perhaps divinely instituted society, but

---

[8] Keller and Goetze, *Hans Sachs,* 23: 271-303.
[9] Ibid., p. 283.

this is belied by their content. Lobwasser was quite capable of presenting a way of life only to point out with the refreshing directness peculiar to him that it should not exist at all, as in "Nonnen":

> Die armen Nonnen/
> Gantz vnbesonnen/
> Beredt sind wordn/
> Zu gehen in Ordn/
> Gotts dienst zu treiben/
> Vnd Keusch zu bleiben/
> So doch offt mehr/
> Ihr Zucht vnd Ehr/
> Gewart bey ihren Freunden wehr.
>
> (no. 16)

Nor was Lobwasser uncritical of the authority of his own faith's clergy. Perhaps the following epigram reflects his feelings on the difficulties which we know his psalter encountered in the Lutheran church; it was fully accepted only in the Reformed Church. But beyond such a biographical detail, in "Evangelische Prediger. New Priester" he was engaging in the hard-hitting, stubborn polemics of a generation that was unwilling to substitute a new orthodoxy for the old one:

> Die New Priestr/
> Durch New Registr/
> Viel Rechnung machn/
> Zu grossen Sachn/
> Seind in der blüe/
> Ist noch zu früe/
> Doch wird geacht/
> Dass sie sich sacht/
> Anmassen werden Bapstes Macht.
>
> (no. 18)

Despite this critical, modern attitude, sometimes he insisted with medieval piety on maintaining the status quo of the estates: "Es soll niemand/ Schreiten aus seinm Beruff vnd Stand" (no. 25). Perhaps these contradictions are resolved in the following epigram, "Vnterthan," in which Lobwasser summarily stated the Lutheran attitude toward authority:

Den Vnterthan/
Ich dess ermahn/
Dass er allzeit/
Der Obrigkeit/
Gehorsam leist/
Wie das Gott heist/
Fürcht ihr Gewalt/
Doch der Gestalt/
Dass er Gott mehr für Augen halt.

(no. 35)

Lobwasser's staunch Lutheranism is significant not only in analyzing his own work but also in understanding the polemical epigram in general. This type of satire was quite different from rhetorical, or manneristic, satire, which had for its subject stock characters and their vices and which addressed itself to a highly literate audience. The polemical epigram expressed a point of conscience, whereas the manneristic epigram experimented with a form of expression. In the polemical epigram the content mattered more than the form, for it was a child of the Reformation, essentially anticourtly and popular. It often contained a vehement attack on specific abuses, usually social, that were limited to Germany, whereas the targets of the rhetorical epigram were standard for all European humanists.

The development and increasing sophistication of the polemical epigram may be indicated by a comparison of four pieces written over a period of more than a hundred years. They all deal with the theme of the corruption of the clergy by worldly goods, a standard theme of Lutheran literature. The first quote is a rather prolix prose lamentation from Agricola's proverb collection (no. 734):

Im anfang der Christlichen Kirchen seindt wenig Stiffte, Clöster, vnd Clausen gewesen, vnd vil Christen, jetzt seind vil Kirchen, Clöster, Stiffte, vnd Clausen, ja alle winckel voll, vnd seindt wenig Christen.

A primitive and rather humorless antithetical construction in the arrangement of "then / now," "many / few" justifies Agricola's classifying this piece as a proverb. Equally straightforward and inelegant is Hans Sachs's "Münich," one of his rare critical descriptions of a calling:

> Wir münich vor uralten jaren
> Ainsidel und waltprueder waren,
> Lagen in andechtig gepet
> Mit fasten, wachen frue und spet,
> Hoften, dadurch selig zu werden.
> Doch leb wir icz anderst auf erden:
> Mancherley orden, rott und seckt,
> Da nicht vil gaistes inen steckt. [10]

Sachs's verse is a little more sharply phrased than Agricola's prose, but the statement it contains is as generalized as Agricola's. There is no trace of wit or of a deliberate progression leading to a point. In contrast, Lobwasser's technique in "Höltzern Bischoff" is clearly epigrammatic:

> Die Bischöff warn/
> Gülden vor Jahrn/
> Der Stab ohn Pracht/
> Von Holtz gemacht:
> Itzt kompts gar ab/
> Der Bischoffs Stab/
> Der hat vil Golts/
> Köstlich vnd Stoltz/
> Die Bischöff aber sind von Holtz.

> (no. 10)

Instead of speaking generally of the enrichment of the clergy, Lobwasser focused on a single item, the bishop's staff. The choice is particularly fortunate, since any item of clerical clothing is intrinsically symbolic and may therefore effectively perform a second function, such as symbolizing clerical corruption. The arrangement is antithetical as in the other two examples. But instead of the simple juxtaposition of past and present, rich and poor, pious and corrupt, now gold and wood are played out against one another in a semimagical, almost alchemistic sleight of hand as one material turns into another. In the last line, a well-prepared metaphor, the bishops appear as wooden puppets, figures of ridicule.

The fourth and latest treatment of the same theme was written in the far more sophisticated idiom of the seventeenth century. The

---

[10] Ibid., p. 300.

dual themes of the lost purity of primitive Christianity and the present clerical corruption continued to haunt the consciousness of the later period; however, Logau expressed them in the now fashionable alexandrine in "Kennzeichen der wahren Kirche":

> Der mit dem Beutel gieng, hiess Judas; der zu legen
> Sein Haupt nicht hatte Raum, heist Christus. Zeitlich Segen
> Ist lange nicht die rechte Lieverey,
> Zu kennen, wer ein Christ in Christus Kirche sey.
>
> (I, 5, 25)

The tradition of social criticism is clearly continuous, even though the language has become much smoother and its power of expression much subtler. The quiet change of tense in the first two lines is very effective: Judas ("hiess") is a historical figure; Jesus ("heisst") is the living Christ. Logau belonged to a generation that had become conscious of the poetical possibilities inherent in grammatical structure. Still, it is clear that even in the seventeenth century Luther cast a long shadow over a literary genre that is all too often considered the sole domain of Martial, Opitz, and their followers. The polemical epigram provided a meeting ground for Reformation and Renaissance, and the result was peculiarly German.

Religious, or theological, polemics not only continued from the sixteenth into the seventeenth century but took on fresh vigor, at least in the epigram, now that the German language had become more pliable and expressive. Logau wrote some of his finest polemics on the subject of forced conversions, a burning issue that never ceased to arouse his indignation. He commented on it more acutely and bitterly as his style became ever more complex. Among his earliest epigrams we find "Gottesdienst ist ohne Zwang."

> Wer kan doch durch Gewalt den Sinn zum Glauben zwingen?
> Verläugnen kan zwar Zwang, nicht aber Glauben bringen.
>
> (I, 2, 98)

The subject of the sentence in the second line is "Zwang"; "Verläugnen" and "Glauben" are both objects. In simple prose the sentence would read: "Zwang kann zwar Verläugnen bringen, aber nicht Glauben." Logau inverted the statement in such a way that the position of emphasis before the caesura is held by "Gewalt" in the first line, "Zwang" in the second. The latter half of both lines is dominated by "Glauben," and thus the stress falls on the incompatibility of faith and force. The double rhyme ("Glauben zwingen / Glauben bringen") puts a further stress on this dominating substantive. The infinitive, so long withheld and now bolstered by the rhyme, gives the verse its ring of authority. Another, later example of the same theme is "Glaubens-Zwang":

> Den an Aposteln stat bekehren die Pistolen,
> Glaubt anders offenbar, glaubt anders dann verholen.
>
> (I, 5, 74)

The word "offenbar" is used here not in the usual sense of "obvious" but rather as "out in the open." Hence the second line means: "He professes one thing in public and believes another in private." The antithetical pair "offenbar / verholen" is matched in the first line by the rather startling and original "Aposteln / Pistolen," which, except for the *a, i,* form a perfect anagram. The anachronism must have sounded quite humorous at a time when pistols could still be considered the latest in modern warfare. The assonance of the two words would, of course, have delighted any Baroque ear.

The point of all these epigrams is that persecution for the sake of Christianity involves an intrinsic contradiction. Logau expressed this again and again with jarring images and clashing propositions. "Gewaltsame Bekehrung" is from his later years:

> Wann durch tödten, durch verjagen, Christus reformiren wollen,
> Hett ans Creuz er alle Juden, sie nicht Ihn, erhöhen sollen.
>
> (III, 2, 87)

The force of this epigram depends on the vision of Christ as crucifier, in other words, a vision of Christianity turned upside down. The image is reenforced by the swift succession of the subject-object pair in the second line: "er alle Juden / sie nicht Ihn." This clash is a perfect fusion of content and imagery. Yet it would be wrong to think of Logau as "enlightened" or tolerant in an eighteenth-century sense. His faith was distinctly not of the Enlightenment, and what at a superficial glance seems tolerance has nothing to do with the easy indifference of a later period. Rather than looking forward to the Enlightenment, Logau's faith harks back to the humanistic past; it could be described as a kind of Erasmian piety, a humanistic Lutheranism. Like Erasmus, Logau insisted on a live, vibrating, and charitable Christianity, not hidebound by dogma but revealing itself in every action of daily life. Since some of his witch-burning contemporaries were apt to stand on dogma to the exclusion of charity, the poet wrote his famous "Glauben":

> Luthrisch, Päbstisch und Calvinisch, diese Glauben alle drey
> Sind vorhanden; doch ist Zweiffel, wo das Christenthum dann sey.
>
> (II, 1, 100)

He did not claim that all religions are equally good but pointed out that they may all become equally bad.

He was himself a convinced Lutheran who occasionally quoted verbatim from Luther, as in the title of I, 2, 86: "Ich bin, wer ich bin, so bin ich dess Herrn." Many of his poems attest to his concern with the finer points of theology, and these constitute still another portion of his polemical writings. Here are two on the priority of faith over works:

> Glaube
> Ein Bau von Stahl, von Stein und Eichen,
> Darff langer Zeit nicht leichtlich weichen;
> Ein Bau, der auff dem Glauben steht,
> Vergeht, wenn Ewigkeit vergeht.
>
> (I, 3, 47)

> Das Blut Christi
> Ich wag und glaub es nur, dass Jesus Christus Blut,
> Zu tilgen meine Schuld, sey gar genug und gut;
> Wer will, der wasche sich durch eigner Wercke schwitzen;
> Im sterben wird man sehn, was Blut, was Schweiss wird nützen.
>
> (II, 7, 57)

To denigrate the value of good works, Logau used the homely "schwitzen" (suggestive of a steam bath?) in contrast to the patently more valuable blood of Christ. "Gute Wercke" is more complex and, in its circumlocutions, more "baroque":

> Dass Gott mir durch sein Werck in mir den Glauben stärcke,
> Für diess Werck gelten nichts viel tausend meiner Wercke.
>
> (I, 4, 83)

That is, man's faith is God's work; hence man's work is as nothing in comparison with ("für") his faith, which is divinely made and instilled.

Two or four lines are enough to make a forceful assertion of an accepted doctrine, as we have seen. But it is far more difficult to argue a subtler point of theology within the same limits. This is what the later Logau did, when he took on the question of the relevance of good works in spite of the priority of faith. In solving the resulting difficulties he showed himself once again to be a master epigrammatist, as in "Glauben und Wercke":

> Hastu einen Engels-Glauben, treibstu aber Teuffels-Wercke,
> Glaub ich gar nicht, dass dein Glauben, die du vorgibst hat die Stärcke.
>
> (Z 142)

Good works will not bring salvation, but they will show the quality of a person's faith: the point is made with the utmost succinctness. In "Der Christen Stern-Deutung" the rationalist joined the Protestant as Logau rejected astrology in a proudly humanistic gesture of reliance on man and his faith alone:

> Christen dörffen nicht Planeten;   (dörffen = brauchen)
> Ihre Wercke sind Propheten,
> Ietzt zu Segen, ietzt zu Nöthen.
>
> (Z 195)

In these later poems Logau seems to have been grappling with the growing narrowmindedness and self-righteousness of some of his fellow Protestants and the accompanying repressiveness of the church. In "Der Glaube" his point was that pure faith could not be a justification for a soiled conscience and impure conduct:

> Mancher wil in Glaubens-Sachen reiner sich als andre schliessen;
> Gut! obs wahr, da lasse reden seinen Wandel und Gewissen.
> Denn auss Wandel und Gewissen
> Kann man erst den Glauben schliessen.
>
> (III, 4, 13)

The older Logau again and again pleaded for an active Christianity. The relationship between faith and works is expressed incisively in "Christenthum":

Christenthum besteht im Thun; drum so bitt ich um Verlauben,
Dass beym Glauben, der nichts thut, ich nicht darff dem sagen glauben.

(ZD 32)

At the same time, despite his criticism of his fellow Protestants, there can be no question about Logau's Protestant loyalty. His anti-Catholic epigrams leave no doubt on that score. In particular, he frequently accused the Catholics of abusing their doctrine of free will to such an extent that it became an excuse for licentiousness. "Free will" may also lead to the atrocities of war, as he showed in "Der Catholische Mars":

Unser Will ist ietzt gebunden,
Krieger-Wille der ist frey;
Mars beweiset alle Stunden
Dass er gut Catholisch sey.

(I, 6, 52)

In addition to the obvious attack on free will, the idea of making a Roman god into a good Catholic is a typically Protestant barb pointed at the Catholic worship of a multitude of saints. In "Der freye und knechtische Wille" Logau pronounced the doctrine of free will, as conceived by the Catholics, to be effeminate, fit only for women, unworthy of men:

Männer sollen luthrisch glauben; Weiber wollen bäpstisch seyn;
Männer solln den Willen binden; Weiber wollen ihn befreyn.

(III, 6, 98)

The "Männer / Weiber" contrast is clear; more subtle is the juxtaposition of "sollen / wollen." Their association and position in the poem give these two normally subordinate verbs theological meanings — a sober sense of duty and capricious waywardness, respectively.

Neither polemics nor epigrams remained one-sidedly Protestant efforts. The Catholics returned the charges with the same weapons. About twenty years after Logau expressed his doubts about the whereabouts of Christianity among the various creeds, the distinguished Catholic poet Johann Scheffler, the Silesian Angel, the mystic *par excellence* among epigrammatists, wrote the following bit of totally humorless polemics, "Allein der katholsche Christ ist weise":

> Miss dir nicht Weisheit zu, wie klug du dir auch bist,
> Niemand ist weis in Gott als ein katholscher Christ. [11]

But perhaps humor was impossible for Scheffler, whose religious conviction was unquestionable when he wrote the fifth and particularly the sixth books of the *Cherubinischer Wandersmann*. While there is some difficulty in establishing which of the earlier books were written before and which were written after Scheffler's conversion to Catholicism, there can be no question about the sixth book: it was written by an adamant convert. [12] These poems are not meant for a small group of intimate friends joined in the pursuit of God and the Good Life — the congenial Franckenberg circle, for whom the first books were written. [13] On the contrary, the epigrams of the sixth book are fragments of a hellfire sermon tossed into a sinful world that deserved to be hated if it refused to be saved. This is the poet who became a fanatic and urged that recalcitrant heretics, namely Protestants, should be killed without mercy. [14] The tone of these poems is coarse, the weapon blunt and heavy:

---

[11] *Der Cherubinische Wandersmann*, book VI, number 253. Subsequent references are to book and epigram numbers. In spite of its immense popularity, no really good edition of the *Cherubinischer Wandersmann* exists. I am using the most recent edition of Scheffler's poetical works, *Angelus Silesius. Sämtliche Poetische Werke in drei Bänden*, ed. Hans Ludwig Held (Munich, 1949), vol. 3. This edition is a somewhat mixed blessing, because of its inconsistently updated orthography. However, it is likely to be the standard edition for years to come, and recent work on Scheffler is based on it. For a discussion of its advantages and drawbacks, see Max Wehrli in *Anzeiger für deutsches Altertum und deutsche Literatur* 66 (1952-1953): 140-42.

[12] For all matters pertaining to the external circumstances of Scheffler's life, I am relying on Georg Ellinger, *Angelus Silesius. Ein Lebensbild* (Breslau, 1927) (hereafter cited as *Angelus Silesius*).

[13] The deeply pious Franckenberg is reported to have felt himself above, or rather at the heart of, all creeds. Asked to which church he belonged, he replied: "Ego sum religionum COR, id est catholicae, orthodoxae, reformatae." Ibid., p. 54.

[14] "Sein 'Gerechtfertigter Gewissenszwang' (1673) tritt für die Berechtigung der zwangsweisen Ketzerbekehrung ein. Ketzerei als das schlimmste aller Verbrechen müsse auf jede Weise ausgerottet werden; man trage ja auch schließlich kein Bedenken Wölfe, Mörder und Diebe in der Verteidigung niederzumachen." Hans Heckel, *Geschichte der deutschen Literatur in*

Des Teufels Schlachtvieh
Die Seele, welche sich die Sünde läßt ermorden,
Die ist (o großer Spott!) des Teufels Schlachtvieh worden.

(V, 333)

Das verächtlichste Aas
Wer sich den Teufel läßt erschlagen und ermorden,
Der ist ein toter Hund des schnödsten Schinders worden.

(VI, 49)

Essentially this is the language of the Reformation, even though it is used for Catholic purposes. It is ironic that the language of Scheffler's fanatic poems, unlike the language of the nonpolemical poems he had written as a Protestant, was heavily indebted to Luther.

Antithesis, a device of which Scheffler was elsewhere a consummate master, became so simplified in the sixth book of the *Cherubinischer Wandersmann* that it seems to be a parody of itself, as in "Der Sünder wird zu Kot":

Der Heilge steiget auf und wird ein Gott in Gott,
Der Sünder fällt herab und wird zu Mist und Kot.

(VI, 29)

Yet as one continues to read the sixth book, the drastic sensuality of these verses becomes fascinating because they are so stripped of ornamental devices, so obsessed with their own precision, as in "Die schnödste Dirne":

Mensch, lässt du dich dein Fleisch beherrschn und nehmen ein,
So muss wohl deine Seel die schnödste Dirne sein.

(VI, 51)

Beastliness and excrement are the images with which Scheffler related worldly success to the devil:

Der Sünder hat keine Ehre
Der Sünder ist des Tiers und aller Teufel Stall;
Drum fehlts ihm doch and Ehrn, hätt er sie überall.

(VI, 27)

Schlesien (Breslau, 1929), 1: 293. The pamphlet itself seems to be virtually inaccessible.

> Ein reicher Sünder, ein vergoldter Kot
> Mensch, kein vergoldter Kot ist reich geehrt und schön;
> Die Sünder auch, die gleich in lautrem Golde stehn.
>
> (VI, 28)

Again he used Lutheran imagery. "Luther's grossly concrete image of the anal character of the Devil" as well as the psychological validity of linking gold, excrement, and hell, has been demonstrated by Norman O. Brown in a different context. [15] The essential rightness of such imagery, despite its crudity, makes it easier for the reader to understand that these polemical verses are part and parcel of Scheffler's work and not a mere curiosity. The seventeenth century was not an age whose inward vision ruled out an intense concern with society. Other religious poets wrote pamphlets on the issues of the day; for example, Friedrich Spee wrote "Cautio Criminalis," a polemic against witch trials. Scheffler's last verses exhibit the same imagination that produced the transcendent imagery of the earlier books. If man is linked to the devil through the sight and smell of excrement, he is linked to God through the sight and smell of the rose in "Die Rose":

> Die Rose, welche hier dein äussres Auge sieht,
> Die hat von Ewigkeit in Gott also geblüht.
>
> (I, 108)

Even at such a distance from inscriptions the epigram retained some of its object-oriented qualities in Scheffler's labeling of worldly things, assigning them their places in the households of God and Satan.

Religious struggles provided the main fuel for the polemical epigram. However, there were other types of polemical epigrams. We have seen that *Ständesatire* seems to have been the staple of the earliest epigrams in the sixteenth century. Logau's work provides the most interesting development of the *Ständesatire*. Logau attacked the soldier's calling most frequently, certainly most vehemently, and one should view his epigrams on the Thirty Years' War as criticism

---

[15] Norman O. Brown, *Life against Death: The Psychoanalytical Meaning of History* (Middletown, Conn., 1959), p. 209. See also part 5, "Studies in Anality," passim.

of a particular profession. He attacked the more obvious outrages of soldiers, but he did not attack war as such, at least not so unequivocally that one is justified in making a pacifist of him. The idea of seventeenth-century pacifism is attractive to twentieth-century readers, and hence Logau is often praised in terms that are altogether too modern. For example, Raymond Pissin, in an article written shortly after the end of World War II, treated Logau as if he were a postwar poet of our own time. [16] The temptation to do so is strong when one reads epigrams such as "Der Soldaten gutes Werck":

> Busse zeucht dem Kriege nach; wo das Heer nur hingetreten,
> Thun die Leut als weinen nichts, nichts als fasten, feyern, beten.
>
> (Z 102)

and "Die ietzigen Soldaten":

> Sind Martis Kinder nicht feine, gesegnete Leute?
> Was Gott, Mensch, Feind, Freund hat, wird ihre tägliche Beute.
>
> (I, 1, 52)

But to concentrate on these verses — and there are not very many of them — is to obscure the fact that Logau also presented the soldier in positive terms, as in "An einen kriegerischen Held" (I, 1, 42), and that he pointed out the distinction between good and bad soldiers, as in "Soldat, durch Versetzung: als tod":

> Soldaten sind ein Volk, die durch beherzte Thaten
> Der Welt und ihrem Thun viel dienen und viel rathen.
> Wann aber ein Soldat der Welt dient wider Gott,
> Der bleibt, indem er bleibt, ist, eh er bleibt, als tod.
>
> (I, 3, 8)

While he certainly did not show much love for the military profession, neither did he deny its usefulness. The epigrams that deal with the outrages of war are better poems than those that balance the attacks, yet it is anachronistic to read into them a complete rejection of war per se without considering their connection with the poetic tradition of castigating the various estates.

---

[16] Raymond Pissin, "Friedrich von Logau und die Gegenwart," *Berliner Hefte* 1 (1946): 539-43.

Another type of polemics to which the modern reader is thoroughly accustomed is the political. The epigram would seem to be particularly suitable for themes of a purely secular and public nature, yet actually such poems are very rare in the work of seventeenth-century poets. Logau wrote no epigrams dealing with specific political questions. Czepko, however, whose poems are among the most interesting and most underrated of the period, worked subtly and precisely with political issues. For example, "Mit der Saüle, das Gebaüde. An Deutschland":

Ich sag es, Deutschland, dir sol Oesterreich ja fallén,
  Wie jedem seinen Fall der Himmel auserkiest:
Du fällst mit ihm: ich hör, ich höre Haüser schallen,
  Dann mit der Saülen fällt, was drauff gebauet ist. [17]

This epigram deals with the dependence of one political entity on another in terms of the interdependent parts of a building. Contrary to custom, Czepko did not make a moral judgment, but concentrating on his subject, he simply made a political prediction in poetic terms. In the following epigram, "Wallensteinischer Tod," Wallenstein's title, Duke of Friedland, gave Czepko an opportunity to pun on the general's activities:

Der alles wust allein, was er durch andre that,
  Und zwar von Friedland kam, doch Krieg und Streit erhaben:
Liegt ohne Titul dar. Fragstu, wer ihn begraben?
Deutsch weiß ich's nicht, sonst heist es la raison d'Estat. [18]

The deliberately placed foreign phrase at the end of the stanza is probably meant to stress Wallenstein's opportunism: he played a political game with no regard for the welfare of Germany and was buried by his own ambitions, summed up by a cold French term for which there is no German equivalent ("deutsch weiß ich's nicht"). Czepko was virtually the only epigrammatist who treated politics in this manner, that is, in secular terms only. Perhaps the political corruption of seventeenth-century Germany caused the educated, epigram-writing classes to turn in despair from what must

---

[17] Czepko, *Weltliche Dichtungen,* p. 367.
[18] Ibid., p. 382.

have seemed hopeless situations. Whatever the reason, the fact remains that a confrontation with public issues was not the primary interest of German Baroque poets, who concentrated instead on questions of language and means of elegant expression, concerns that will be discussed in the next chapter.

Toward the end of the century Christian Wernicke introduced another variant of the polemical epigram, the epigram of literary criticism. [19] Rhymed criticism was not new in Europe. In France Wernicke was preceded by Boileau, whose *L'Art Poetique* (1674) he knew and admired. Wernicke's own epigrams appeared in three editions, 1697, 1701, and 1704. [20] In England Pope's verse *Essay on Criticism* was to appear in 1711. But Wernicke was the only notable practitioner of verse criticism in Germany; there the fashion never caught on, perhaps because Opitz had written his criticism in prose, and others followed him in this as in so many other areas.

To the modern reader Wernicke is chiefly of interest as a transitional figure at the end of the Baroque period. But Lessing thought more highly of him than of any other German epigrammatist and ranked him close to Martial. The following passage is worth quoting because the subject inspired Lessing to a considerable flight of fancy:

Wer ihm [i.e., Martial] aus allen Zeiten und Völkern, noch am nächsten kömmt, ist unser Wernicke. Beider Reichtum ist fast gleich groß: nur daß man dem Reichtume des Deutschen ein wenig zu sehr die Mühe und den Schweiß ansieht, den er gekostet. Martial gewann den seinigen unter Menschen und von Menschen: Wernicke förderte seinen, oft nicht ohne Lebensgefahr, aus dem Schoße der Erde zu Tage. Wernicke besaß mehr von den Metallen, woraus Geld zu münzen: und dem Martial ging mehr gemünztes Geld durch die Hände. [21]

With his usual acumen Lessing commented on a certain uninspired quality of Wernicke's work ("der Schweiß, den er gekostet"). He was probably more impressed by Wernicke's lucidity and critical

---

[19] See Wernicke, *Epigramme*. Pechel, in his pedestrian but valuable introduction, surveyed not only Wernicke's life but also the literary background.

[20] See ibid., pp. 61-73, for differences between these editions.

[21] Lessing, *Werke*, 14: 155.

talent than by his ability as a poet. And Lessing was right: what Wernicke wrote stands between the seventeenth-century epigram and the prose essay and aphorism of the eighteenth century. Wernicke frequently added prose comments to his epigrams as if he were not quite at ease with either form. Yet his verse is fluent and correct, and he demanded these qualities of other epigrammatists. Establishing and maintaining proper literary standards is, in fact, his main theme, as he declared in "Auf den Lauf und Fall Französcher Verse":

> Wer Vers' in Franckreich schreibt, der schreibet ohne Zwang,
> Hüpft über Berg und Thal, als über kurtz und lang;
> Pflegt in dem schnellen Lauf das Ohr oft zu vergessen,
> Und weiß die Sylben nur zu zehlen, nicht zu messen:
> So daß kein Vers gefällt, es sey, daß er ihn liest,
> Ihm einen leichten Schwang im Lesen weiß zu geben;
> Und, weil er seinen Thon halb sinckend weiß zu heben,
> Ein besserer Poet, als der Verfasser ist.
>
> (IX, 4)

Although this is a fairly long epigram, it cannot contain its theme, which spills over into a prose comment about twice the length of the poem. In the following epigram, "Auf ein gewisses Sonnet," the poetic form proves less of a handicap because Wernicke parodied what he censured:

> Es schreibt Pirecles ein Sonnet,
> In welchem der Verstand in steter Irre geht;
> In welchem nach der letzten Zeilen,
> Die dreyzehn erstere wie in ihr Wirtshaus eilen.
> Denn ist gleich weder falsch, was vorhergeht, noch wahr;
> So ist der Endspruch dennoch klar:
> Er schleußt durch ein grob Wort, sein dunckeles Gedichte;
> Und spritzt die Feder aus, dem Leser ins Gesichte.
>
> (IX, 16)

"Ursprung und Fortgang der Teutschen Poesie" is a summary of German literature at the end of the century:

> Den Deutschen Pegasus setzt' Opitz erst in Lauf,
> Und Gryph verbesserte, was an ihm ward getadelt;
> Hernach trat Lohenstein mit Hoffmanswaldau auf,
> Die unsre Dichter-Kunst, und sich durch die geadelt!

Die setzten Zierd' und Pracht zu jenes Eigenthum;
Der hat den ersten zwar, doch die den grössten Ruhm.

(VII, 63)

Opitz was still the lawmaker of German poetry; although Wernicke was opposed to *Schwulst,* he was sufficiently steeped in the taste of his time to admire the most baroque of Baroque poets, Lohenstein and Hofmannswaldau. Yet he praised them in the measured, sober tones of the eighteenth century.

After Wernicke the epigram declined rapidly, despite Lessing's interest in it and his own epigrams. As the poetic qualities that distinguished the seventeenth-century epigram came to be less and less in demand, the polemics of a later age took other forms. The epigram became an uninteresting vehicle for witticisms that could just as well be conveyed in prose. Indeed, no eighteenth-century epigrammatist could compete with the great aphorist Lichtenberg. When Schiller and Goethe wrote their *Xenien,* the seventeenth-century tradition had been broken and they did not revive it; instead they made a new form out of a new and different appreciation of the ancients.

CHAPTER IV

RHETORIC AND MANNERISM IN THE EPIGRAM

THE VAST MAJORITY OF SEVENTEENTH-CENTURY SATIRICAL EPIGRAMS are neither polemical, nor side products of the Reformation, nor weapons in the struggle of ideas; rather, they arise from an entirely different tradition, Neo-Latin poetry. This is hardly surprising when one considers that the epigram was a favorite form among the Latin poets in Germany, as elsewhere. A recent comprehensive study of the Neo-Latin tradition states: "Es gibt kaum einen Lyrikband der Neulateiner, der nicht auch Epigramme enthält." [1] Under the direct influence of Martial and in the wake of the curiously inflated reputation of the Scotsman John Owen, as well as others, epigrams were written in Latin and later in German to attack stock vices and foibles. The targets were the cuckold, the miser, the dishonest lawyer, the old coquette, and so on. The anonymity of the characters was further emphasized by their frequent retention of Latin names. These epigrams constituted a kind of elegant verbal fencing: they were not meant to draw blood but to demonstrate and exercise the writer's skill. Their prevalence and their patent tendency to imitate existing patterns have earned for the seventeenth-century epigram in

---

[1] Karl Otto Conrady, *Lateinische Dichtungstradition und deutsche Lyrik des 17. Jahrhunderts* (Bonn, 1962), p. 166. The passage continues: "Ihr Themen- und Motivschatz ist nicht sonderlich groß; darauf kommt es auch nicht an. Vielmehr gilt es, dem Gedanken die gutsitzende, pointierte Form zu verschaffen.... Mit der poinierten Prägung des Gedankens stellt sich oftmals antithetische Gedankenführung ein.... Keineswegs aber ist die Kunst der Pointierung auf das Epigramm beschränkt; sie ist innerer Bestandteil der gesamten neulateinischen Lyrik."

general a reputation of slavish unoriginality and repetitiveness. Yet this was the kind of writing that the theorists encouraged; therefore the modern reader does well to withhold judgment and examine the poets' own esthetic assumptions first. This has not always been done. On the contrary, the few existing discussions of individual epigrams go emphatically in the other direction, like so much of the older criticism of Baroque poetry. Under the heading "Wanderungen eines Epigramms" Waldberg traced a typical series of repetitions. [2] The theme is a dog barking at thieves but keeping quiet for lovers, thus serving both his master and his adulterous mistress. This theme, it appears, can be found in the work of individual poets and in anthologies, with only slight variations. [3] Waldberg's conclusion is a wholesale condemnation of poets who engaged in this and similar exercises: "Den Poeten aus der ersten Hälfte des siebzehnten Jahrhunderts gehen vor allem zwei für jede künstlerische Leistung selbstverständliche Voraussetzungen ab, das ist die Wertschätzung der künstlerischen Originalität und die Achtung des fremden geistigen Eigentums." [4]

Waldberg's judgment was based on an anachronism. He did not perceive that originality is not in question here: the poet was working in a tradition based on the time-honored discipline of rhetoric. A poet who wrote within this tradition would not only have felt free to draw on its "storehouse of topoi" [5] but may actually have felt obliged to do so. He was continuing the topical literature of the Middle Ages, the literature of the significant commonplace. If it seems remarkable to find these ideas operating at so late a date, it should be remembered that the schools encouraged the habit of

[2] Waldberg, *Renaissance-Lyrik*, pp. 211-14.

[3] It is amusing to compare this use of dogs in Baroque poetry with another, almost diametrically opposite use, shown by Blake Lee Spahr in "Dogs and Doggerel in the German Baroque," *Journal of English and Germanic Philology* 54 (1955): 380-86. By concentrating on the human qualities of canines in satirical poems, Spahr shows how the identification of man and dog could lead to a high degree of originality, verging on disguised autobiographical self-irony.

[4] Waldberg, *Renaissance-Lyrik*, p. 205.

[5] "Im antiken Lehrgebäude der Rhetorik ist die Topik das Vorratsmagazin." Ernst Robert Curtius, *Europäische Literatur und lateinisches Mittelalter* (Berne, 1948), p. 87.

rhetorical thinking, particularly in the writing of epigrams. Furthermore, as late as 1711 we find Pope's well-known lines:

> True wit is nature to advantage dressed,
> What oft was thought, but ne'er so well expressed. [6]
>
> (*Essay on Criticism,* lines 297-98)

By Pope's time this "well expressed" thought had become something
that was widely familiar and was about to be superseded.

A rhetorical epigram, then, is one in which a concept is given
new and, if possible, more elegant shape. By using a theme with
which his audience was familiar, the epigrammatist could direct attention to his rhetorical abilities, whereas an unfamiliar and
provocative idea would have distracted from the performance itself.
If the thought could be found in the ancients, so much the better.
In any case, "what oft was thought" was taken for granted and
only the expression mattered. In fact, it showed special skill if one
idea could be used for opposite purposes, such as for encomium
and for censure. Two examples from Opitz will illustrate this point:

> Du sagst, es sei der Spiegel voller List
> Und zeige dich dir schöner als du bist;
> Komm, wilt du sehn, daß er nicht ligen kan,
> Und schaue dich mit meinen Augen an.

> An eine ungestalte Jungfrau
> Aus dem Griechischen Lucilii, lib. II,
> Anthol. tit. εἰς δύξειδεις

> Die Spiegel sind ganz falsch; dann wann sie richtig weren,
> Du würdest dir zu sehn in keinen nicht begehren. [6]

The topos of the false mirror image serves in both instances, now
positively, now negatively. Opitz's careful reference to his source
in the second epigram indicates his intention to use a conventional

---

[6] Martin Opitz, *Ausgewählte Dichtungen von Martin Opitz,* ed. Julius
Tittmann, Deutsche Dichter des siebzehnten Jahrhunderts, vol. 1 (Leipzig,
1869), pp. 60 (no title), 64. Some interesting general speculations on the
subject of *elegantia* and its relation to the epigram can be found in Preisendanz, *Spruchform,* part 1.

image and is not to be confused with modern meticulousness about footnoting. Seventeenth-century poets sometimes did and sometimes did not credit their sources. To accuse them of intellectual dishonesty when they did not is misdirected indignation because the matter was not of ethical but only of esthetic importance. If the source was venerable, as in the case of the *Anthology,* it might be interesting to the reader and would therefore add to the prestige of the poet to mention it; otherwise there was no point in being specific about one's *fontes.* Besides, the well-educated reader was supposed to recognize the source. As a basic rule, the concept of plagiarism did not yet exist, but it is worth observing that there were occasional attempts at developing the idea, although with no great consistency. An example is the following verse by Georg Greflinger, who was himself certainly no *Originalgenie*:

> Du schmückest dein Gedicht mit eines andern Müh,
> Opitzens Verse sind das Fette von der Brüh,
> Wird dieses abgeschöpft, wer will das ander fressen? [7]

The rhetorical tradition accounts for much. However, it is perhaps worth questioning whether it can fully account for the peculiarity of a concept of satire that does not primarily aim at the castigation of the object satirized. Modern taste, schooled in the satire of Voltaire, Swift, and their followers, finds it difficult to imagine any other standard for satire than effective attack. But as we turn to the critical underpinnings of Renaissance and Baroque epigrams, what emerges beyond any doubt is the precept that the good satirical epigram should not be sharp but merely well delivered, that it should not hurt but merely delight. The emphasis on the padded blow in the interest of good taste has not received sufficient attention by modern scholars. Opitz's definition of the epigram has been quoted on pages 27 and 28; two other passages about the epigram may serve as evidence for the contention that good satire was supposed to be harmless and painless. The three passages were written by Germans over a period of almost two hundred years, thus showing how deeply ingrained this view of satire was. Beatus Rhenanus

---

[7] Urban, *Owenus,* p. 39.

wrote the following passage in 1518 as a dedication of Sir Thomas More's Latin epigrams to Willibald Pirckheimer in Nuremberg. He praised More as a consummate epigrammatist, then continued:

Nam elegantissime componit et felicissime vertit. Quam fluunt suaviter huius carmina! Nihil hic durum, nihil scabrum, nihil tenebricosum. Candidus est, argutus, Latinus. Porro gratissimam quadam festivitate sic omnia temperat, ut nihil unquam viderim lepidius. Crederim ego Musas quicquid usquam est iocorum, leporis, salium, in hunc contulisse. Quam lusit eleganter ad Sabinum ale inos pro suis tollentem liberos! Quam salse Lalum ridet, qui videri Gallus tam ambitiose cupiebat! Sunt autem huius sales nequaquam mordaces, sed candidi, melliti, blandi, et quivis potius quam amarulenti. Iocatur enim, set ubique citra dentem; ridet, set citra contumeliam.

(For he composes most tastefully and translates most happily. How pleasantly his poetry flows! How utterly unforced is his work! How adroit it all is! Here is nothing harsh, nothing rough, nothing obscure. He is bright, sharp, a master of Latin. Furthermore he seasons his work with a certain very delightful humor so that I have never seen anything more charming. I could believe that the Muses conferred upon him all there is anywhere of mirth, charm and wit. How gracefully he pokes fun at Sabinus for bringing up another's children as his own. How wittily he ridicules Lalus, who went to such lengths in his desire to seem French. And yet his witticisms are by no means ill-natured, but rather are honest, sugar-coated, mild, anything but bitter. He provokes laughter, but in every case without pain; he ridicules, but without abuse.)[8]

The passage is worth reading in its entirety because it sets forth admirably the Renaissance desiderata for a writer as exemplified by an epigrammatist. Beatus Rhenanus defined excellent writing as suave, elegant, and mellifluous. The key word, "elegant," occurs twice in this passage. In the Renaissance the concept of *elegantia* applied not only to a style of writing but also to a style of life. [9] Clearly, however, such requirements are in conflict with the true satirist's intention, which is certainly not to avoid offending his victims. Thomas More is in effect praised for being harmless. This preference for harmlessness is evident also in Beatus Rhenanus's choice of examples: Sabinus and Lalus, the cuckold and the fob, are straw

---

[8] Thomas More, *The Latin Epigrams of Thomas More,* ed. and trans. Leicester Bradner and Charles Arthur Lynch (Chicago, 1953), pp. 4, 126.

[9] Preisendanz calls *argutia* the "integrierende Element" of *elegantia,* which points "nach innen auf eine Gesinnung, nach außen auf einen Stilwillen." *Spruchform,* p. 30.

puppets, exemplifying standard literary situations. Such terms as "candidi, melliti, blandi," hardly apply to Lobwasser's verses about pilfering artisans and corrupt clergymen or to Logau's epigrams against fanatics.

The latest piece of criticism is Wernicke's "Beschaffenheit der Überschriffte," an epigram about epigrams:

> Dann läßt die Überschrift kein Leser as der Acht',
> Wenn in der Kürtz' ihr Leib, die Seel' in Witz bestehet;
> Wenn sie nicht allzutieff mit ihrem Stachel gehet,
> Und einem Abriss nur von einer Wunde macht....
>
> (I, 1)

In a characteristic comment Wernicke added: "Die Satyrische sind ohnstreitig die besten Überschriffte, es müssen aber keine Schmäh-Schrifften seyn." [10] At the very threshold of the Enlightenment, the beginning of the great age of satire, the old insistence on the padded blow still existed.

It is evident that under these circumstances the targets of satire were relatively unimportant and the traditional stock characters of vice and folly would do as well as or better than any others. It should be clear that there was nothing accidental about the imitativeness and repetitiveness of what I have called the rhetorical epigram. These elegant variants of rebuke fulfilled the demands and standards of their time. They did what they were meant to do: reflect and counterreflect depersonalized, stereotyped human behavior, like mirrors reflecting wax figures.

Closely related to the rhetorical impulse and to some extent growing out of it are the experiments in form with which seventeenth-century poetry abounds. However, many of these did not aim at what was most appropriate and fit, that is, the rhetorical writer's goal of classic elegance, but rather at unusual expressions and hitherto untried images. They must be classed as manneristic. The value placed on striking and startling expression should not be confused with a concern for original content, which was simply not an issue in either manneristic or rhetorical practice. The differences

---

[10] Wernicke, *Epigramme*, p. 133.

between rhetorical and manneristic epigrams are not as great as they appear. The seventeenth-century epigram admirably illustrates Curtius's dictum that an exaggeration of rhetorical ornamentation leads to mannerism and that rhetoric therefore contains the germ of mannerism. [11] We are dealing with a continuous spectrum which ranges — often within the work of one poet — from classic dignity and simplicity to rather extreme and labored experiments with form. The decision as to where mannerism starts along this scale is often a matter of personal taste.

One of the major accomplishments of the seventeenth-century epigram is its demonstration of the possibilities of the alexandrine. The terseness of the epigram emphasized the antithetical principle inherent in the alexandrine, whereas the greater content of a longer poem or a play tended to suppress the effect of the single pair of lines. Trunz has commented on the significance of the alexandrine in seventeenth-century literature:

Für das Barockjahrhundert war es der Vers, den man brauchte. Seine Klarheit entsprach dem Rationalismus der Zeit; seine Länge vermochte dem pansophischen Suchen nach Beispielen zu genügen, dazu aller Sprachfreude und allem rhetorischen Prunk; seine Zweiteiligkeit kam der Spannung von Diesseits und Jenseits, Zeit und Ewigkeit entgegen, die das ganze Weltbild beherrschte. [12]

The last statement can be illustrated with a few lines from Czepko's *Monodisticha*. [13] Deeply fascinated with antithesis, Czepko often used it in first lines as well as complete verses:

Wie Gott Mensch wird, so wird der Mensch hingegen Gott.

(I, 29)

---

[11] "In der Rhetorik selbst liegt also ein Keim des Manierismus verborgen." Curtius, *Europäische Literatur und lateinisches Mittelalter*, p. 276. See also the ensuing discussion on the relationship of rhetoric and mannerism in the Middle Ages, pp. 276-83; and Gustav René Hocke, *Manierismus in der Literatur* (Hamburg, 1957).

[12] Erich Trunz, "Die Entwicklung des barocken Langverses," *Euphorion* 39 (1938): 468. The article is marred by occasional lapses into Third Reich jargon, appearing, as it did, at a time when *Euphorion* went by the name of *Dichtung und Volkstum*.

[13] Daniel von Czepko, *Geistliche Dichtungen,* ed. Werner Milch (Breslau, 1932). Subsequent references are to epigram numbers; Roman numerals indicate groups of hundreds.

Wer Gott empfängt, verliert auch Gott.

(I, 31)

Der Tod löst auf: die Lieb hingegen setzt zusammen.

(I, 74)

Die Seele schleust den Leib, der Leib die Seel in sich.

(I, 95)

Mensch kleide dich in Gott: Gott wil sich in dich kleiden.

(II, 67)

The caesura accomplishes a leap from time to eternity. In an essay on Angelus Silesius Benno von Wiese has commented on this type of religious epigram and its use of the alexandrine: "Welt- und Lebensbild des mystischen Barock enthalten Spannungen und Gegensätze von solcher Weite und Tiefe, daß sie in fast gespenstischem Kontrast zu der Kürze und Knappheit der epigrammatischen Form stehen, in der sie sich aussprechen." [14] More recently a detailed and perceptive study by Elisabeth Spörri has exhaustively treated the poetic possibilities of the alexandrine in Scheffler's work, increasing our understanding of the mechanics of the single alexandrine and hence of the epigram. [15]

But a form-obsessed generation of poets was not satisfied with exploring the alexandrine to its limits. The epigram appears too short to allow for much variation in its form and shape, yet this limitation seems to have been a stimulant rather than a deterrent to Baroque poets. They devised titles that are in themselves epigrams, literally epigrams on top of epigrams. For example, in the first hundred of Czepko's *Monodisticha*: "Wo Stille/ Da Fülle," "Sich hassen/ Alles lassen,/ Gott fassen," "Gottes Gütte/ Feste Hütte." Czepko had used this device in his earlier secular epigrams, for example, "Die Herren schlüßen/ die Bauern büßen." [16] Other poets used it as well; Johann Grob also wrote epigrams as titles

---

[14] Benno von Wiese, "Die Antithetik in den Alexandrinern des Angelus Silesius," *Euphorion* 29 (1928): 504.

[15] Elisabeth Spörri, *Der Cherubinische Wandersmann als Kunstwerk*, Zürcher Beiträge zur deutschen Sprach- und Stilgeschichte, no. 2 (Zurich, 1947) (hereafter cited as *Der Cherubinische Wandersmann*).

[16] Czepko, *Weltliche Dichtungen*, p. 366.

for epigrams: "Unbesonnen freien bringet langes reuen," "Man wird ohne Creuzes plagen/ Wenig nach dem Himmel fragen." [17] And there are unusual visual arrangements. Again Czepko's titles are a good example:

```
Anfang     Ende
        im
Ende       Anfang (I, 1)


Alles     Nicht
       im
Nicht     Alles (I, 40)


Sterben:    Leben:
         ist
Leben:      Sterben (II, 10)
```

Considering the content, one has the impression that Czepko thought a systematic arrangement of words could help him chart the infinite, a notion that is fully in keeping with the intense rationality of his epigrams, somewhat like that which inspired Pascal's *Pensées*. Harsdörffer, another poet who used visual effects, built a *Stammbuchvers* around the word *Gemüt*, intersecting it as a cross: [18]

```
        G
        E
    G E M Ü T
        Ü
        T
```

Even more striking is Logau's "Alles auf GOTT":

```
Mir nicht, wann ich bin geboren, bin ich sondern meinem  ⎞
Mir nicht, wann ich wieder sterbe, sterb ich, sondern meinem ⎟
Mir nicht, wann ich etwas habe, hab ich, sondern meinem     ⎬ GOTT
Mir nicht, wann ich etwas werde, werd ich sondern meinem  ⎠
```

                                                    (II, 8, 54)

---

[17] Johann Grob, *Epigramme*, ed. Axel Lindqvist, Bibliothek des literarischen Vereins in Stuttgart, vol. 273 (Leipzig, 1929), pp. 139, 166.

[18] Keil, and Keil, *Deutsche Stammbücher*, p. 102.

The title has two meanings: all the lines on the paper lead to the word "GOTT" just as all the events in a man's life lead to God's presence.

It was in such purely religious poems that Logau experimented most extensively with form and most clearly proved himself a seasoned Baroque poet. He employed devices that are usually found only in longer poems. For example, in "Undanck gegen GOTT" he used what Curtius calls a *Summationsschema*: [19]

> *Gott* hat seinen Sohn gesand, uns zu retten auß der *Noth*;
> *Noth* hat seinen Sohn erbarmt, drum zu leiden bittren *Tod*;
> *Tod* wird schlecht von uns bedanckt, mehrenteils mit Fluch und *Spot*;
> *Spot* darff leichte rechnen so ewig mit *Spot, Tod, Noth, Gott.*
>
> (II, 8, 52; italics mine)

The scheme is similar to the sestina but is packed into the narrow framework of four lines. The last word of each line becomes the first word of the next. The last four words of the last line repeat the first words of all four lines, but in reverse order, so that the poem ends with its first word. Such repetition causes a certain relaxing of the attention. In a long poem it may lead to boredom and inattention on the part of the reader. But here the substantives denoting eternity — "Gott," "Tod" — slide into and merge with those denoting earthly misery — "Noth, "Spot." Together they evoke a scene in which heaven and earth grapple with one another in an ever-repeated crucifixion. If the subject of the poem were longer, the closely meshed interaction of the words would lose its impact.

Logau's "Das Werck der Erlösung" is similar:

> *Gott* was bin ich gegen dir! Nichts als ein eitler *Koth*;
> *Hohn* und Tod wie daß dann mir lied zu Nutz dein *Sohn*? (lied=litt)
> *Bloß* die Liebe hats gemacht, die mir Erden-*Kloß*
> *Heil* von Sünden hat gebracht und am Himmel *Theil.*
>
> (II, 8, 53; italics mine)

Here the first word of each line rhymes with the last word of the same line. It is a curious fact that the ear will not pick up this rhyme, even on a second and third reading and even if the neces-

---

[19] Curtius, *Europäische Literatur und lateinisches Mittelalter*, p. 293.

sary adjustments between long and short vowels are made. The effect is therefore largely visual, or perhaps it would be better to say intellectual; the achievement is one of visual symmetry rather than sound. But an additional rhyme tying the half-lines together is clearly audible. Obviously the intention was to juggle as many verbal effects as possible in as tight a space as possible. Considering the subject of the verse, the poet is somewhat in the position of a juggler before the Lord, a pose that is quite compatible with the humility he professes.

Still another epigram by Logau, "Gott dient allen; wer dient ihm?" has some features of a sonnet:

Gott schafft, erzeucht, trägt, speist, tränckt, labt, stärckt, nährt, erquickt,
Erhält, schenckt, sorgt, beschert, vermehrt, gewehret, schickt,
Liebt, schützt, bewahrt, erlöst, beschattet, benedeyt,
Schirmt, sichret, führt, regirt, errettet, hilfft, befreyt,
Erleuchtet, unterweist, erfreut, sterbt und erweckt,
So daß sich fort und fort sein Heil auff uns erstreckt.
Mit allem dienstu, Gott, uns allen! ist auch wol,
Der dir dient, einer nur und dient dir, wie er sol?

(II, 2, 76)

A break occurs after the first six lines, and the last two lines draw a conclusion from the previous ones; the effect is that of a so-called Shakespearean sonnet with its concluding couplet. Unlike the sonnet this poem consists entirely of couplets, but the break is nevertheless distinct not only in content but also in form: in the last lines the choppy cumulation of verbs is abandoned in favor of a more complex syntax and the smoother flow of a question. The overall impression is of a shorthand sonnet, a kind of abbreviated poetic form that occurs frequently in Gryphius's work. Also typical of Gryphius is the technique of cumulation, or *Häufung,* which in Logau's poem suggests the limitless, breathtaking bounty of God. [20]

---

[20] Marian Szyrocki speaks of the "fact" that Gryphius's epigrams influenced Logau to some extent and that the influence was mutual: "Umgekehrt hat sich Gryphius in seiner Epigrammausgabe von 1663 aber auch von Logau inspirieren lassen." Marian Szyrocki, *Andreas Gryphius, sein Leben und Werk* (Tubingen, 1964), p. 74 (hereafter cited as *Andreas Gryphius*). The statement is brief, tantalizing, and undocumented. I know of no external evidence that would substantiate it, but, on the basis of internal evidence, I am inclined to think that it is probably correct and could be worked out in some detail.

This surprising variety in the structure of the epigram is partly due to the fact that in the seventeenth century the epigram was still seen as closely related to sonnets, madrigals, and other longer forms. The reader will remember Opitz's uncertainty as to what constituted an epigram, as well as the Renaissance "doctrine of equivalence" whereby the Italian and French small forms, particularly the sonnet, were equated with the Greek epigrams of the *Anthology*. A glance at Zincgref's collection of 1624 will further corroborate this point. His *Auserlesene Gedichte deutscher Poeten,* an appendix to his edition of Opitz's works, was intended to show that there were other good poets besides Opitz then writing in Germany. Of its fifty-two poems almost half are Zincgref's own. W. Braune pointed out that the collection contained new imports from abroad — the epigram, the sonnet, and the ode. [21] He failed to point out, however, that what passed for epigrams in Zincgref's anthology betrays the compiler's considerable ignorance concerning the nature of the genre. Number 24, a poem by Caspar Kirchner entitled "Epigramma," is actually a love song of four stanzas. The printer ran them together but they are clearly separable, especially since each stanza ends with a refrain. Even the broadest definition of the epigram cannot admit such a stanzaic poem. Number 26, Zincgref's "Epigramma vom Thurn zu Strassburg, warumb der andere darneben nit auffgebawet worden," consists of three quatrains (*a b b a*) joined through enjambment. Only two lines short of a sonnet, the poem exemplifies the close connection between epigram and sonnet. Perhaps Zincgref called it an epigram because the subject reminded him of inscriptions on buildings. Number 44, also by Zincgref, is entitled "Epigramma: was der recht Adel sey"; it consists of three quatrains (*a b a b*), this time without enjambment, thus showing even more clearly a division into three stanzas. On the other hand, number 22, Caspar Kirchner's "An Herrn Jörg Kobern Medicinae Doctorn," is an epigram although it is not called "Epigramma," and occasionally we find the title "Überreime" in place of "Epigramma," as in number 2 and number 49. There are also a few satirical epigrams in Zincgref's collection.

---

[21] Julius Zincgref, *Auserlesene Gedichte deutscher Poeten, gesammelt von Julius Wilhelm Zinkgref, 1624,* ed. Wilhelm Braune, Neudrucke deutscher Litteratur-werke, vol. 15 (Halle, 1879), p. vi.

All this points to the fact that the origin of the German epigram was no more and no less than a firmly structured lyric poem. Neither its exact form nor its content was prescribed, despite Opitz's suggestions that it should be a short satire. The result was a far greater range of poetic possibilities than was the case in later times, when the epigram came to be more and more a statement distinguished, literally, by rhyme and reason alone.

It is well known that devising puns and anagrams of all kinds was a favorite pastime of seventeenth-century literati. Therefore it is not surprising to find them in both religious and secular epigrams. But while it is customary to treat religious word games with respect, their secular equivalents usually meet with a more than equal amount of contempt. [22] This contempt can be traced back as far as Wernicke, who wrote an epigram, "Auf das Wörter-Spiel," on the subject:

> Daß keine schlechte Wort' ein Pegnitz-Schäffer spricht;
> Daß er die Freud' und Lust der Sinnen Sonne nennet,
> Und vor ein Stirn-Gestirn der Phillis' Aug' erkennet,
>   Verwundert mich im Minsten nicht:
>   Denn, wenn an diesem fruchtbarn Ort,
> Wo schnatternd alle Gäns in Schwanen sich verkehren,
> Parnassus schwanger ist; so pflegt er zu gebähren
>   Statt einer Mauss, ein Zwilling-Wort.

(V, 4)

Fifty years earlier Logau had defended the practice of punning in "Mit Worten spielen":

Ist es gut mit Worten spielen
Schad und Nutz kan nicht vervielen (vervielen = multiplicare. Eitner's note)
Wer gewinnt, der wird betrogen;
Wer verleuret, hat gelogen.

(I, 7, 18)

Logau himself punned on the word "spielen," using it to mean both "play" and "gamble," thus emphasizing not only the playful but also the deceptive element of what appears to be harmless verbal trickery. Although Logau approved and Wernicke disapproved of

---

[22] See for example Hudson, *The Epigram*, p. 156.

punning, they agreed that it was a game of no great importance. Nevertheless, it is worth asking whether the kind of poetic word analysis practiced in the seventeenth century was as innocuous and trivial as it appears at first sight.

Seventeenth-century literature was affected by the impact of a philosophy of language derived from Böhme and his sources; this included the concept of a *lingua adamica* and the idea that words are not accidentally formed but are expressive of the thing they designate. Paul Hankamer wrote: "Wörter sind in ihrer eigentlichen Wurzel Gebilde der schaffenden Natur. Die Dichtung ist nicht eigentlich Werk des menschlichen Geistes. Wir spielen und tändeln und künsteln mit der übermenschlichen Natursprache.... Buchstabenspielerei ist Spiel mit den Dingen selbst, ist bedeutungsvoll; denn Wort und Ding stehen in magischem Bezug."[23] Hankamer, who quotes Schottel and Zesen, among others, shows that these ideas were widely held in the seventeenth century. The problem is to determine, within the limits of our context, how seriously and by whom they were held. Perhaps nothing makes such demands on the critic's or scholar's sense of historic tact than the linguistic sensibilities of the past. One cannot be perfectly sure what undercurrents and overtones a word or phrase was meant to convey. A certain amount of punning was, of course, simply a matter of eloquence, a demonstration of mastery of the language and the rules of rhetoric. But this does not go far enough to explain the obsessive seriousness in the seventeenth-century approach to word games. The explanation proposed here, admittedly hypothetical and depending on an empathetic reading of the poetry in question, is that the idea of a *lingua adamica* was the background of all the word and letter games of the period, both secular and religious, without which they become meaningless. (Indeed, they were considered meaningless by generations of critics who shrugged them off as incomprehensible nonsense.) On the other hand, one would go much too far in assuming that every one of them is a deliberate demonstration of Böhme's *Natursprachenlehre.*

---

[23] Paul Hankamer, *Die Sprache. Ihr Begriff und ihre Deutung im sechzehnten und siebzehnten Jahrhundert* (Bonn, 1927), p. 118 (hereafter cited as *Die Sprache*).

The concept that language has more meanings than strictly
logical or rational ones is not new to twentieth-century readers. But
where we interpret psychologically, the seventeenth-century reader
interpreted metaphysically. While we must beware of confusing
these two approaches, we may profit by an analogy. In modern
poetry, words are frequently used in a context of free association
pointing to certain unconscious or semiconscious connections, a
practice that would be incomprehensible to a reading public that did
not have at least a nodding acquaintance with the discoveries of
depth psychology. Nevertheless, we cannot read modern poems as
nothing but illustrations of certain Freudian concepts of language,
nor can we assume that the reading public has accepted such concepts
completely and unquestioningly. Such a complex intellectual situation
is clear to us as contemporaries of modern poems, but it is far from
clear in the case of poems written three hundred years ago. [24] We
cannot re-create the intellectual atmosphere in which the word games
were written. Yet even without knowing the exact balance, we may
safely assume that both playfulness and seriousness entered into
the writing of these poems and that the playfulness increases and the
seriousness diminishes as we move from religious to secular poetry.

Böhme's views were well known in the Franckenberg circle to
which both Czepko and Scheffler belonged. [25] Virtually possessed by
logomania, Czepko went further than any other epigrammatist in
attempting to stretch the word to the limits of its meaning, as in the
epigram "ICH":

> J. Gott.   C. Christus.   H. Das ist der Heilge Geist:
> Mensch, wann du sprichest: ICH: Schau, wo es dich hin weist.
>
> (VI, 95)

This verse contains a poetic, and in that sense a playful, interpretation of a word and its letters: the self contains a suggestion of God

---

[24] Consider, for example, the mixture of amusement, irritation, and
recognition one feels in encountering a line such as Peter Viereck's "The poet
wears neurosis like new roses." In two hundred years the words and the pun
will presumably be as clear as they are now, but who will understand the
calculated sophistry of their effect?

[25] Ellinger, *Angelus Silesius,* p. 65.

in the components of its name, *i, c, h,* even as man himself possesses a spark of the divine. Elisabeth Spörri, on the other hand,
proposes that Czepko seriously believed that the letters *i, c, h* were
a symbol for the trinity. [26] But the words "Schau, wo es dich hin
weist" are suggestive rather than definitive and can be taken to
mean, "Consider these lines as a meaningful game." This attitude
of playfulness may also be observed in the following epigram, which
sports three puns and an elaborate title:

> Eva: Ave:
> Adem: Made:
> Natur: Natter
> Hätt Eva nicht erlangt durch Ave eine Cur:
> Wär Adem Made noch, und Natter die Natur.
>
> (III, 47)

That Eve and Mary complement one another is supposedly expressed in the very name *Eva.* But even if Czepko was serious about
the transposition of the first word, how could he continue to be
serious when he had to tamper with *Adam* and change *Natur* in a
somewhat less than obvious way? Is it not more likely that truth,
in a scientific sense, is not even attempted? In that case, the study
of Böhme opened the door to a vast domain which the poet was
free to explore but not obliged to analyze as a scholar. Given this
freedom, Czepko's etymology becomes extremely ingenious, ranging
over the ancient languages as well as modern German:

> M. ENS. CH.
> Mensch, das Wort Mensch sagt dir: was vor ein Mensch du bist.
> Im Wort, in dir ist MENS: ist ENS: was mehr? ein Christ.
>
> (VI, 50)

> M....ens
> M....eins
> Ens: Das gemeint dich Mensch: Mens sondert dich in dir:
> Denn Mens das bringt mein Ens, und Meins mein Einst herfür.
>
> (VI, 69)

---

[26] "Er glaubt ernstlich an die metaphysische Deutbarkeit von Wörtern
und Buchstaben.... Zum Beispiel sieht er in den Buchstaben ICH das Zeichen
der Trinität." Spörri, *Der Cherubinische Wandersmann,* p. 50.

The poet's didactic tone and the fact that he was playing with ultimate questions make these games appear more philosophically solid than they are. As soon as the tone ceases to be didactic, the carelessness and lightheartedness of the etymology become immediately apparent, as in Logau's "Das Weinacht-Fest," even though the subject is still religious and must be taken seriously:

> Kümt vom Weinen, kümt von Weihen, kümt vom Wein Weinachten her?
> So wie ieder ihm sich brauchte, kamen sie ihm ohn Gefehr.
> Weil der Welt-Erlöser drinnen in die Welt is kummen ein,
> Solten sie Frei-nachten heissen, solten sie Freu-nachten seyn.

> (III, 4, 92)

The rhyming and alliterating syllables are played out against each other solely to create a mist of inebriated happiness. In the second line the reader is implicitly asked to take his pick of possible interpretations. The last two lines perform a somersault of verbal joy, transforming linguistic irresponsibility into a total affirmation of God's Christmas gift to man. Despite its highhanded treatment of etymology, the poem loses a good deal of its charm if one fails to realize that it was composed in an age that believed in the God-given significance of words.

Transpositions or anagrams were the most common type of word game. Logau used these liberally and for a variety of purposes. In criticism of the upper classes—to which he belonged—he wrote "Hofe-Leute, versetzt: hohe Teufel":

> Hofe Leute, hohe Teufel; ist es nicht zu viel gesaget?
> Nein, weil mancher arme Leute sehrer als der Teuffel plaget.
> Falschheit und Betriegligkeiten, Hinderlist, Verleumdung, Lügen
> Seind dess Hofes Meisterstücke, sind deß Teuffels sein Vergnügen

> (II, 3, 22)

Against the *à la mode Wesen* he wrote "Parole, versetzt: O Prale":

> O prale, Landsmann, pral, in fremder Sprache Schmucke!
> Du pralst in fremder Sprach und fremd in deinem Rocke.

> (I, 3, 58)

The latter is one of the very rare instances in which a French word is used in a transposition. Usually the poets limited themselves to

German and Latin, with an occasional sampling of Greek, precisely the languages that the mystics considered, with Hebrew, to be divinely inspired. And Hebrew, of course, was not one of the languages a German poet was expected to know. Here is an example of a Greek-German anagram, Logau's "Reich, durch Versetzung: Cheir":

> Cheir heist Griechen eine Hand,
> Stecket in dem Wörtlein Reich.
> Wer da reich ist, werde gleich
> Einer milden Hand erkant,
> Die da gibet und nichts nimmt,
> Die verschenckt und nichts bekümmt.
>
> (I, 2, 88)

In his late work, at the height of his ability, Logau could shuffle several anagrams at once, as in "Bule, versetzt: Übel; Bulen, versetzt: Beuln":

> Schöner Bule, schnödes Übel, freches Bulen, schlimme Beuln,
> Trifft zusammen, folgt einander, wie auff sichres lachen heulen.
>
> (III, 1, 9)

Further down the road to triviality we find the transpositions of proper names as a form of compliment. These were very common and were usually addressed to a member of the nobility or a patron of the poet. Logau's "An eine fürstliche Person. Ludewig, versetzt: 'Wie Glud'" (II, 9, 70) is an epigram of eight lines in which "Glud" is interpreted as the glow of virtue. It ends: "Fürst und Herr, wie eine Glud brennet immerdar!/ Daß das Feuer und die Glud lesche nie kein Jahr." Clearly the compliment is not a mere tour de force showing the poet's ingenuity. The underlying assumption, whether sincere or not, is that transposition reveals the true nature of the name and hence of the person. An even crasser example of what must appear to the modern reader as not only barefaced but also farfetched flattery is Logau's "Anne Sofie, Hertzoginn, versetzt: Sonne zog in eine Fahrt." Outdoing himself, the poet turned this still another way: "Anne Sofieh, Hertzoginne, versetzt: Geh, o feine Sonnen-Zieraht." (Both anagrams form the title of II, 9, 5.) The spelling is outrageously adapted to the needs of the anagram. Still, since Logau presumably intended to please the recipient, one may assume that the duchess secretly hoped he had revealed the inner mystery of her name and title.

Czepko's epigrams have illustrated an interest in individual letters that was apparently related to sixteenth-century studies of the cabala. [27] Cabalists believed that each letter has a meaning and is capable of revealing divine secrets. [28] These notions entered into poetry but were balanced, and perhaps more than balanced, by the pleasure of alliteration, as in Logau's "Der Buchstabe G.":

Meistens alles auff der Erden, drauff die Leut am meisten streben,
Stehet unter denen Dingen, die sich auff ein G anheben:
Gold, Geld, Gut, Geschencke, Gaben, Gunst, Gewin, Gewalt, Geschicke,
Glaube, Glimpff, Gesund, Gewissen, und mit einem Worte Glücke
Wil sich alles drunter stellen, Wann zu diesem zu sich zehlet
Gott mit seiner Gnad und Güte, weiss ich nicht was Gutes fehlet.

(III, 1, 47)

Close attention to individual letters also led to such unexpected esthetic refinements as Logau's interpretation of vowels in "A. E. I. O. U.":

A.   ist derer, die nicht wollen.
E.   ist derer, die nicht sollen.
I.   ist derer, die da zagen.
O.   ist derer, die da klagen.
U.   ist derer, die da plagen.

(I, 7, 57)

"Für Böhme," Hankamer writes, "haben die Vokale einen Symbolcharakter, der je eine Stufe und Haltung in der ewigen Selbstgeburt Gottes und damit in allem Lebenslauf ausdrückt." [29] Granting that Logau's analysis is a far cry from a mystic interpretation of letters, it does show the vowels as symbolizing different attitudes toward life. In other words this poem has a place on the same symbolic

---

[27] The relation is traced by Wolfgang Kayser in "Böhmes Natursprachenlehre und ihre Grundlagen," *Euphorion* 31 (1930): 521-62.

[28] There are many Jewish legends dealing with the alphabet. According to one of these, the letters existed in the crown of God before the creation of the world.

[29] Hankamer, *Die Sprache,* p. 158.

scale, though at a different point, from a more distinctly mystic view of the alphabet.

There are more eccentric experiments with single letters. The mesostich, for example, consists of letters raised in a sentence to spell another word. A moving variant of this form are Logau's eteostichs, or chronograms, written during the Thirty Years' War. Here, instead of a word, a date is spelled out in Roman numerals. The eteostich for the year 1640 reads:

> GIeb, gIeb Vns FrIeD, O FrieDe gIeb Vns, Gott!
> FrIeD Ist Vns Ia so nVtz, aLs etVVa LIebes Brot.
>
> (I, 4, 73)

Others are "Vom Jahr 1638" (I, 3, 43) and "Das Jahr 1642" (I, 6, 58). If we keep in mind the metaphysical possibilities inherent in single letters, such an epigram assumes something of the quality of an incantation.

The evidence regarding word and letter games seems to point to a continuum of metaphysical meaning extending from the most mystical religious epigrams to innocuous and even trivial secular epigrams. On the other hand, since we are dealing with poetry and not with theology or philosophy, it is probably incorrect to assume that any poet was totally committed to a given philosophy of language. This view is contrary to the usual opinion that denies deep significance in secular word games and stresses it too heavily in religious ones. [30] Word and letter analyses, while they are to some extent best understood as maneristic, also express an underlying, primitive awe for language and a terror of words. Kayser has pointed out that Böhme's age as well as the following century was still full of "Zauber-, Fluch-, Segensworte, Worte jedenfalls, die mit den Dingen natürlichen wenn auch geheimen Zusammenhang hatten. ... Daß davon auch seine Natursprachenlehre mit ihrer Beziehung zwischen dem Wort und dem Wesen, der inneren Natur eines Dinges, irgendwie berührt ist, leuchtet ein." [31] The epigrams we have discussed were written in and for a society that was far too secular and sophisticated to give full credence to primitive magic, and at

---

[30] Spörri, *Der Cherubinische Wandersmann,* pp. 55, 60-62.
[31] Kayser, "Böhmes Natursprachenlehre," p. 552.

the same time too naive and superstitious, perhaps also too God-fearing, to discard the old ties completely in favor of the dawning rationalism. As a result, the instinctive fear and adoration of the word were dressed up in courtly costume, often endowed with humor and cast in an elegant role; yet that role never became quite detached from the original power that Adam gained over the animals when he first called them by name.

CHAPTER V

CONVENTION AND ECCENTRICITY: SCHEFFLER AND GRYPHIUS

THE EPIGRAM, PARTICULARLY THE SEVENTEENTH-CENTURY EPIGRAM, tends to be an anonymous form. The reasons are obvious: a short poem does not permit as much display of individual style as a longer one does, and the rhetorical tradition of bandying a theme back and forth among a circle of initiates tended to obscure the individual poet's identity.

However, one epigrammatist is distinctly recognizable, even to the educated general reader, namely, Angelus Silesius, as the Silesian poet Johann Scheffler called himself. Among the poets discussed in this study Scheffler is the only one who has enjoyed considerable fame not merely for a few scattered verses but for a sizable body of work. Scheffler's modern reputation began with Friedrich Schlegel's edition of *Der Cherubinische Wandersmann,* first published in 1820. Significantly, the full title of this edition reads, *Anfangspunkte des christlichen Nachdenkens nach den Sprüchen des cherubinischen Wandersmanns,* [1] indicating that nothing was farther from Schlegel's interests than Baroque poetry. He frankly used Scheffler's verses as a framework around which to drape his own ideas: "Die tiefe Wahrheit, welche diese Gedanken in sinnereicher Kürze und oft mit überraschender Klarheit enthalten, bildet sie mir zu bequemen Stützpunkten, oder vielmehr zu hellen Lichtpunkten, um die eigenen

---

[1] Friedrich Schlegel, *Anfangspunkte des christlichen Nachdenkens nach den Sprüchen des cherubinischen Wandersmanns (1820),* ed. Hans Ludwig Held (Munich, 1917).

Gedanken daran zu reihen." [2] Typical of Schlegel's incomprehension, unconcern, or perhaps simply dislike for the exigencies of the alexandrine is the fact that he rearranged it to fit into four lines, starting a new line after the caesura. This creates a superficial impression of a folk song stanza and causes considerable formal confusion: the pauses are lengthened, the rhythm is changed, and false enjambments are created.

Schlegel's inadequacies as an editor would be of no importance in this context were it not that he seems to have started a trend. Down to our own time there has been a tendency to see Scheffler outside the context of his period and his fellow poets as someone who was unique in kind, not only in quality. It has for a long time been common knowledge—indeed, it is indisputable—that Scheffler drew heavily on sixteenth-century mystics, even borrowing specific images, and that in his form and phrasing he was equally indebted to Czepko, whom he knew personally and without whose *Monodisticha, Der Cherubinische Wandersmann* could not have been written. Nevertheless, as late as 1952 an early essay by Karl Viëtor was republished in which the author claimed to see the beginning of *Erlebnislyrik* in Scheffler's work, a statement as anachronistic and as detrimental to our understanding of Baroque poetry as Schlegel's rearrangements of the alexandrine were. [3] And much of the current work on Scheffler continues to resemble Schlegel's in the sense that the poet is discussed as an independently thinking mystic whose verses can be treated in a modern philosophic context with no reference to or even general awareness of the seventeenth-century background. [4]

How does Scheffler actually fit in with the other epigrammatists of his time? This is the obvious question to ask, for within the context of this study *Der Cherubinische Wandersmann* must be seen

---

[2] Ibid., p. 12.

[3] Karl Viëtor, "Johann Scheffler," in *Geist und Form* (Bonn, 1952), pp. 53-64; first published in *Schlesische Lebensbilder,* vol. 3 (Breslau, 1928).

[4] Joachim H. Seyppel, "Freedom and the mystical union in *Der Cherubinische Wandersmann*," *Germanic Review* 32 (1957): 93-112. Horst Althaus speaks of Scheffler's "religiöse Bekenntnisdichtung." Horst Althaus, *Johann Scheffler's "Cherubinischer Wandersmann": Mystik und Dichtung,* Beiträge zur deutschen Philologie, vol. 9 (Giessen, 1956), p. 71. A good introduction in English is provided by Jeffrey L. Sammons, *Angelus Silesius* (New York, 1967).

as one book of Baroque epigrams among many others, distinct only in quality. But there is little support for this statement. Cysarz, it is true, speaks briefly of "mystische Epigramme." [5] Merker-Stammler's *Reallexikon* specifically states that Scheffler did not write epigrams; it does not, however, attempt a definition of what he did write or a distinction between it and the epigram. [6] Elisabeth Spörri, in her otherwise excellent book on Scheffler, draws a sharp and unconvincing line between the worldly epigram on the one hand and the religious epigram of Czepko and Scheffler on the other. [7] She even claims that Scheffler deliberately did not call his poems epigrams. This is a mistake: he did call them *Schlussreime* in the first edition, a word which was a common equivalent for epigram. The error is even clearer with Czepko's *Monodisticha*. Single distichs were the preferred epigrammatic form of the Greeks and of some Romans; hence in calling his collection monodistichs Czepko clearly thought of his pairs of alexandrines as equivalent to the epigrams of the ancients. Furthermore, he wrote worldly epigrams before he wrote religious ones and the latter are a stylistic outgrowth of the former. Since there are often exact correspondences between Scheffler and Czepko, the relation of Czepko's *Kurtze Satyrische Gedichte,* his secular epigrams, to Scheffler's *Der Cherubinische Wandersmann* exemplifies the connection between secular and religious epigrams.

The confusion regarding Scheffler's place in seventeenth-century literature is compounded by the fact that few scholars would deny the existence of bona fide religious epigrams. Such a denial would indeed be difficult because it would necessitate finding a new category for a large number of epigrams by Gryphius, Logau, Wernicke, and many others. Hence it cannot be demonstrated that Scheffler's subject matter makes his verses something other than epigrams. Nor can it be proven that Scheffler is a mystic while the others are not, and this is perhaps the most important point to understand. The arbitrary separation of Scheffler from his contemporaries obscures the fact that toward the middle of the century and after, mystic subjects were popular among epigrammatists of all kinds. The common domain from which themes and topoi were drawn was not

---

[5] Herbert Cysarz, *Deutscher Barock in der Lyrik* (Leipzig, 1936), p. 94.

[6] "Ganz auf den Spruch beschränken sich die mystisch-katholischen 'Sinnreime' Schefflers." Merker and Stammler, *Reallexikon,* 1: 375.

[7] Spörri, *Der Cherubinische Wandersmann,* pp. 55, 60-61.

limited to satire and love poetry but also included religious subjects; indeed, there are enough excellent poems on religious subjects alone to justify the practice of imitation. Scheffler's work is part of a homogeneous body of poetry, and Miss Spörri is wrong to see it as "den Abschluß einer geistlichen Sprachkunst, während das Epigramm weltlicher Dichter neben und nach ihm fortblüht." [8]

It is a curious but common mistake to assume that mystic poetry must necessarily be the direct result of mystic experience, or that a poet who wished to describe a personal religious experience had no stock phrases and stock imagery on which to draw. The opposite is true: in the seventeenth century, mystic commonplaces abounded. (I am, of course, using the term commonplace in a technical not a pejorative sense, and I do not mean to imply that such commonplaces were platitudes.) The paradox, in particular, had been highly refined and was available to any skillful poet who wanted to give an intimation of the ineffable by means of a complex formulation that would yield only to a close reading. Many successful mystic epigrams employing paradox are wholly or partially derivative, and many were written by poets whose reputation is based on their secular not their religious work. The paradoxical formulation was as available to the religious poet as the marinistic conceit was to the love poet, and often one writer would try his hand at both devices. The following two epigrams, for example, are both by Logau. There are three possible sources for the first, four for the second: [9]

> Dreyerley Tod: deß Fleisches, deß Lebens und der Seele
> Wer nicht eh stirbt, als er stirbt,
> Der vertirbt, wann er vertirbt.
>
> (I, 6, 16)

> Die Geburt ist der Tod; der Tod ist die Geburt
> Der Tod ist nicht der Tod; der Tod ist die Geburt.
> Durch diese kam ich kaum, so must ich wieder fort.
> Der Tod ist nicht der Tod; er ist das rechte Leben,
> Drauß ich mich mehr nicht darf in Ewigkeit begeben.
>
> (I, 6, 79)

---

[8] Ibid., p. 48.

[9] According to Denker, *Logau,* the possible sources are the collections of Heidfeld, Zincgref, and Owen for I, 6, 16; and Heidfeld, Lehmann, Egenoff, and Tscherning for I, 6, 79.

Even the much maligned John Owen wrote mystic epigrams employing paradox, and his German imitators followed him in this as in everything else. Owen wrote:

> Morte tua letum deletum, mortua mors est.
> Crederet at mortem quis potuisse mori? [10]
>
> (III, 78)

Logau's excellent adaptation belies Urban's contention that the imitation of Owen "wirkt nivellierend auf Sprache, Erfindung und Versbehandlung": [11]

> Da das Leben gieng und starb, fing das sterben an zu leben;
> Dann der Tod hat durch den Tod in den Tod sich müssen geben.
>
> (II, 4, 3)

Neither Logau nor Owen has a reputation as a mystic poet, yet they both handle religious paradox competently.

The same is true of Wernicke who, as we have seen, was almost a poet of the Enlightenment. His religious epigrams exhibit the same ease and elegance characteristic of his others, and he seems to have considered the use of paradox as mandatory for a religious theme, as in "Und alle Gräber werden beweget werden":

> Es wird die Wiege zwar, doch nicht das Grab bewegt,
> In das man unsers Leibs entkernte Schalen legt;
> Doch wenn der Lebens-Fürst erscheinen wird, und wenn
> Die donnernde Posaun erschallen wird auf Erden,
> Denn wird das Grab bewegt, und unser Grab wird denn
> Der Neugebohrnen Wiege werden.
>
> (III, 2)

Another of his epigrams, "Schiffahrt des Lebens," uses one of the most timeworn metaphysical images coupled with a self-contradictory conclusion to indicate the incongruity of man's temporal and his eternal substance:

> Wir sein der Wellen Gauckelspiel,
> Weil wir den Hafen nur erreichen wenn wir sincken.
>
> (IV, 15)

---

[10] See ibid., p. 49, for the reference to Owen's epigram.
[11] Urban, *Owenus,* p. 33.

As a true religious poet, Wernicke did not attempt to reconcile reason and faith but rather stressed their incompatibility, as in "Auf die Geburt unsers Heylandes":

> Daß Gott zum Kinde wird, und Allmacht ihren Sitz
> Bey der Verwesung nimmt, geht über meinen Witz:
> Doch beth ich das Geheimnüs an,
> Obgleich ich's nicht begreiffen kan;
> Ich glaub' einfältiglich was niemand nicht ergründt;
> Gott und mein Glaube wird zu einer Zeit ein Kind
>
> (II, 33)

And on the mystery of the sacrament, "Gedancken bey dem H. Abendmahl":

> O Seelig! wer so speißt, daß er, vom Tod' erwecket,
> Was unbegreifflich fühlt, und das Geheimnis schmecket.
>
> (IV, 18)

In this context the work of Angelus Silesius can be seen to constitute neither an unmatched undertaking nor an end of the religious epigram. (Wernicke's epigrams appeared about fifty years after *Der Cherubinische Wandersmann*.) Scheffler's appeal through the ages has probably rested on his peculiar artistic tact. A master of baroque poetic devices, he used them far less obtrusively than his contemporaries did. If one had to define his poetic virtues in a single word, one would want to speak of *mâze*. That this should be true of a poet whom, in another context, we have come to know as a fanatic is another paradox in an age of paradox.

Scheffler's best poetry is outstanding for its clarity and precision, and it often appears to have a certain natural grace when it is actually extremely sophisticated. Poets such as Czepko bent and forced the language to their purposes, whereas Scheffler adjusted to it as he found it. In "Der unerkannte Gott" he reverses all the reader's expectations, yet he does so in a lucid and untortured manner, avoiding verbal shock effects:

> Was Gott ist, weiss man nicht. Er ist nicht Licht, nicht Geist,
> Nicht Wahrheit, Einheit, Eins, nicht was man Gottheit heisst.
> Nicht Weisheit, nicht Verstand, nicht Liebe, Wille, Güte,
> Kein Ding, kein Unding auch, kein Wesen, kein Gemüte.
> Er ist, was ich und du und keine Kreatur,
> Eh wir geworden sind, was er ist, nie erfuhr.
>
> (IV, 21)

Describing God in an entirely negative way, Scheffler reverses the ordinary positive relationship of the epigram and its object. He thus creates a kind of antiepigram, for where the ordinary epigram offers knowledge or perception, this epigram describes the absence of perception, a condition of utter ignorance. For four lines the poet denies that God's essence lies in any of the attributes by which He is usually described. In the last two lines he turns about and speaks of man through the ingeniously simple device of introducing himself and the reader ("ich und du") into the poem. After the seemingly hopeless beginning he now proffers hope of the highest order, a possible union with God; yet this hope, too, is stated in negative terms. The intellectual texture of the poem is mystic-manneristic, but the overall effect is not, because of the plain language and smooth rhythm. The same pattern occurs in Scheffler's mystic interpretation of single letters. This, too, is clearer and less involved, as in "A B ist schon genug," than it is in the poems discussed in the preceding chapter:

> Die Heiden plappern viel, wer geistlich weiß zu beten,
> Der kann mit A und B* getrost vor Gott hintreten.
>
> (II, 77)
>
> *ABBA [Scheffler's note]

This is a rather odd situation in which a complex word game is used in praise of simplicity. *A* and *B* symbolize not only God the Father, as the poet's note suggests, but also forthrightness, implying that he who says *A, B* uses the alphabet in an orderly unpretentious fashion, which in turn leads straight to God. The next verse, "Das Herze," is in the tradition of the emblematic epigram; however, Scheffler does not interpret an elaborate or farfetched image as the emblem does but rather the easily accessible phenomenon of the heart's supposed physiological shape:

> Mein Herz ist unten eng und obenher so weit
> Daß es Gott offen sei und nicht der Irdigkeit.
>
> (II, 82)

When he employs paradoxical imagery it stands out clearly in an uncluttered verse. Again, the image of the heart in another "Das Herze":

Mein Herze, weil es stets in Gott gezogen steht
Und ihn herwieder zeucht, ist Eisen und Magnet.

(III, 132)

All these examples from Scheffler have been chosen to show that *Der Cherubinische Wandersmann,* at least in its first three or four books, presents a moment of balance between rhetoric and mannerism. Scheffler's achievement lies not in his uniqueness and even less in his originality. Nor does his work adumbrate a later type of poetry. On the contrary, his greatness is peculiarly Baroque in that he found the final form, the smoothest polish, for what others had used earlier — the religious commonplace, in the best sense of the term.

Anyone familiar with seventeenth-century German poetry will not be surprised to find that there is one truly original body of epigrams and that their author is Andreas Gryphius. These epigrams would deserve special attention if only for the sake of their famous author, even if they were not as good as they actually are, and yet they have been surprisingly neglected. The prevalent opinion continues to be that of Cysarz: "Die Epigramme ... sind das am stärksten zeitgebundene Stück des Gryphschen Werks"; [12] and that of Hans Heckel: "Die Epigramme sind nur Nebenwerk." [13] In his monograph on Gryphius, Marian Szyrocki has tried to awaken some interest in the epigrams but offers no analysis. Moreover, he dismisses the religious epigrams with a misjudgment: "Man fühlt aber, daß er in diesen Epigrammen, die fast jegliche subjektiven Töne vermissen lassen, seine alte lyrische Kraft verloren hat." [14]

Gryphius wrote three books of epigrams, each containing about 100 poems. The majority of the epigrams in books II and III of the 1663 edition are secular and largely satirical. Book I consists of religious verses that should be read as a unified whole; [15] seen in this manner, it forms a startling and powerful work. The unifying theme of these poems is the incarnation. For the most part they

---

[12] Cysarz, *Deutsche Barockdichtung,* p. 172.
[13] Heckel, *Geschichte der deutschen Literatur in Schlesien,* 1: 243.
[14] Szyrocki, *Andreas Gryphius,* p. 74.
[15] Gryphius, *Oden und Epigramme,* pp. 170-86.

deal with the coming of Christ into a hostile world, but they also deal with the incarnation of man's immortal soul, exemplified by the poet's own soul, into the same hostility and darkness. The second theme, introduced in the earlier epigrams dealing with Christ's birth, vigorously reasserts itself in epigrams I, 61 through I, 70. These ten verses are openly autobiographical, and the parallel between the poet and Christ is drawn with intense candor. Szyrocki's statement merely illustrates that they are hardly ever read, for to my knowledge no other work of Gryphius is so insistently personal. A summary of these epigrams might read: "I, Andreas Gryphius, was born on such and such a date, at the same hour of the night as our Savior. Nor was my experience in a darkened world altogether different from his." This tone is unusual to the point of uniqueness in seventeenth-century epigrammatic art.

Almost at the beginning of the book the theme of the incarnation is introduced in "Uber die Geburt des HErren," not only as a historical fact but as a spiritual situation embodying a theological paradox:

> Der Mensch/ das Spill der Zeit verlohr die Ewigkeit/
> Und Gott der ewig ist nimt an sich Fleisch und Zeit/
> Und trägt der Zeitten Fluch/ den Tod/ daß er das Leben
> Dem was hir sterblich ist auff ewig könne geben.
> So wird/ was noch biß her auf diser Welt gefehlt
> Die Zeitt und Ewigkeit! O Wunderding! vermählt.
>
> (I, 8)

As we proceed through the book it becomes ever more apparent that the poet's concern in this union of time and eternity is with pure spirit descending into filth and crime, pure light submerging itself in darkness, rather than with the opposite, that is, transformation of the body or transfiguration of the darkness. Because he describes the descent of God, not the ascent of man, the birth in the stable illustrates not so much the love of God for man or the humility of Mary as man's beastliness. The innkeeper's refusal to accommodate the holy family at the inn is an example of man's malice, and the stable itself is its symbol. Thus, if God came to search for man, where else would he look for him but among the beasts?

> Der Mensch für welchen Gott ward in der Nacht geboren/
> Hat durch die Sünde/ Licht/ Verstand und Witz verlohren/

> Wen wundert denn das hier bey dunckel voller Nacht/
> Bey Vih' in einem Stall Gott ihn zu suchen tracht'.

(I, 22)

The idea is harsh and startling, the expression terse. The first two lines state a situation and the last two draw a conclusion in the manner later prescribed by Lessing for the perfect epigram. However, the situation is nothing less than the human condition, the conclusion is the prospect of salvation, the objective correlative is a story from the Gospels, and the tone is one of probing, bitter misanthropy.

The theme that God finds no welcome among men is reiterated with several variations. In "Sie hatten keinen Raum in der Herberge" Gryphius, with his unerring sense for contrasts, obtains a striking effect simply by juxtaposing Luke 2:7, "There was no room for them at the inn," with John 14:2, "In my father's house are many mansions":

> Mein Hauß/ die Erden/ Herr hat keinen Raum vor dich/
> In deines Vatern sind vill Wohnungen vor mich.

(I, 14)

Note that this epigram is in the present tense: Christ is born not into the historical past but into the poet's own world. The first word is "mein," the last one "mich," surrounding the birth of Christ with a frame of personal participation. Another epigram on the same subject, "Des HErren Geburt," is in a sense complementary, for it calls on the reader's participation instead of presenting the poet's:

> Der reisend/ unverhofft/ in einem Stall gebohren/
> Der für dich und dein Heil erscheint zu Mitternacht:
> Hat zu der Widerkunfft villeicht die Zeit erkoren/
> Die niemand groß bequem. Mensch nim dich selbst in acht.

(I, 21)

The *du* is obtrusively insistent, the urgency overwhelming; the poet's confrontation with the reader, rather than the poem's occasion, the birth of God, is in the foreground.

The simultaneity of the poet's life and Christ's life is further confirmed in a somewhat longer epigram that uses a conceit frequently found in the hymns of the time. In "Sie hatten keinen Raum in der Herberge" the poet offers his own heart as an "inn" and identifies himself with the suffering Christ child by declaring that he, too, is not fully of and for this world:

> Du komst in deine Welt/ die leider dir zu enge/
> Und Hauß und Platz versagt in rasendem Gedränge.
> Mein Hertz das noch die Welt nicht gantz besessen hat/
> Räum' ich dir Heiland ein zu einer Läger Stadt.
> Mir leider will die Welt auch nicht ein Räumlin gönnen:
> Mit mir/ wirst ausser ihr du dich behelffen können.
>
> (I, 9)

Again and again the poet intrudes on what began as a biblical vignette. In "Des HErren Beschneidung" he addresses Christ in a tone that is virtually envious, as if He were a more fortunate brother:

> Du fängest deine Jahr mit Blut und Thränen an/
> Und endest sie mit Sig und schönem Himmel fahren.
> Werd ich dir denn nicht gleich der stets bey newen Jahren/
> Nichts als new' Angst und Sorg und Elend zehlen kan?
>
> (I, 26)

Although Gryphius claims equal attention for himself, the occasion, at least, for the first sixty epigrams is the life of Christ. But beginning with number 61 and continuing for ten epigrams, he disrupts the biblical context to tell of his own birth. Leaving no doubt that the "I" of these poems is autobiographical, he writes: Über die Nacht meiner Geburt II octob. hora XII p. m." (I, 61). (Gryphius was in fact born on October second.) [16] He returns to Christ and the holy martyrs in numbers 71, 72, and 73: "Geburts Gedancken an Jesum," "Auff den Stern der Weisen aus Morgenland," and "Über die unterirdischen Grüffte der heiligen Märterer zu Rom." But number 74 is again autobiographical:

> Als Glogaw gantz in Grauss verfallen ließ mich Gott
> Beschreiten dise Welt/ nun grimme Krieges Noht
> So Land als Stadt verheert/ ruft Gott mich wieder ein.

---

[16] This is the accepted date. At several points in the poet's work we find the eleventh of October mentioned as his birth date, but this seems to be due to the printer's mistaking the Roman numeral II for the arabic numeral 11. See Szyrocki, *Andreas Gryphius*, p. 120, note 12.

The remaining twenty-six epigrams of the first book deal primarily with the crucifixion. The shift from the divine to the personal and back to the divine, which constitutes the arrangement of the book as a whole, is in keeping with the content of the individual epigrams we have analyzed.

The autobiographical epigrams proper, numbers 61 through 70, retain the analogy to the Christ child that was introduced in the first epigrams, but it is muted now, implicit rather than explicit, as in "Gedancken über meine Geburt":

> Der du mich an das Licht hast bey besternter Nacht/
> Aus meiner Mutter Leib' als einem Kercker bracht!
> Laß fern von Sternen mich/ doch Sternen gleich auffgehen/
> Wenn hir ich untergeh/ dort über Sternen stehen.
>
> (I, 64)

The flesh is darkness, the spirit light, and life takes place in the ambiguity of a starlit night, where the hope of the resurrection precariously balances the anguish of the incarnation. [17] It is characteristic of Gryphius's chiaroscuro imagery that a simple contrast does not suffice; the images are inverted, their meanings are reversed, before they are played out against one another. For example, "Über die Nacht meiner Geburt":

> Diss ist mein erste Nacht/ der Anfang meiner Tage/
> Darin' ich mit viel Angst der letzten Nacht nachjage.
> Doch weil ich meine Nacht Herr durch dein Licht verlohren/
> Bin ich zwar in der Nacht/ doch nicht der Nacht gebohren.
>
> (I, 62)

Positives and negatives chase one another in a circle, taxing the reader's speed of comprehension. It is a highly intellectual poem that appeals to reason while dealing with the basic emotions of hope and terror. "Auff meine Geburt zu Gott" is similar:

---

[17] The ramifications of Gryphius's night imagery are very wide. Here, as elsewhere, I am purposely limiting the discussion to a specific argument. For a fuller discussion, see Gerhard Fricke, *Die Bildlichkeit in der Dichtung des Andreas Gryphius* (Berlin, 1933), particularly pp. 40-43; and Dietrich Walter Jöns, *Das "Sinnen-Bild." Studien zur allegorischen Bildlichkeit bei Andreas Gryphius* (Stuttgart, 1966), pp. 132-39.

Du lissest mich/ da ich nichts war/ geboren werden:
Ach laß mich nicht in nichts nun ich was bin vergehn!

(I, 69)

Here nothingness substitutes for darkness, making even more explicit the terror of the void that dominates all these verses.

Thus the poet sees himself as a participant in the incarnation
of Christ, suffering as Christ suffered from the inhospitality of the
world and the horror of a threatening spiritual vacuum. A human
"I" merges with a divine "Thou," but where the "I" of *Der
Cherubinische Wandersmann* is generic and literary, Gryphius's "I"
is distinctly personal. The union takes place not in a rarefied spiritual
sphere, not in the heaven to which the poet aspires, but in the
filth and pain of the world into which God is born. These poems
are not purely mystical, perhaps not mystical at all since they deal
primarily with the sufferings of the sensitive mind. Gryphius's subject is the anguish of the incarnation, but it is the incarnation of the
human soul, symbolized and epitomized by the incarnation of God.

A brief comment is in order on the form Gryphius employed
in his epigrams. Probably no other epigrammatist was so far removed from the proverb and from popular rhyme as Gryphius;
nor was any other poet so steeped in the taste of his time, even
though, as we have noticed, his epigrams also exhibit a striking in-
dependence, or transcendence, of it. In the epigrams he never de-
parted from the structure of the alexandrine except to employ a
trochaic line of eight beats, related to the alexandrine in its strong
caesura. For example:

Frágt nicht wárumb ích der Wélt/ hóchste Lúst für Únlust áchte/
Frágt warúmb auf wéiter Sée ófft ein Ménsch in Dúrst verschmáchte.

(I, 81)

Such variations are slight and relatively unimportant. Gryphius
remains primarily the master of the alexandrine. More interesting
is the formal connection between his epigrams and his sonnets,
a clear illustration of the so-called doctrine of equivalence of sonnet
and epigram. [18] In no other German poet is the intimate relationship

---

[18] For the historical evidence of this connection and a discussion of its
application to Romance poetry, see Hutton's two studies, *The Greek*

of these two forms more apparent. Sonnet and epigram share a bipartite structure, but in both the Italian and the Shakespearean
sonnet the expository part is longer than the concluding part,
whereas in the epigram the two parts tend to be of equal length.

Gryphius often used a kind of transitional form, a semisonnet
in which the concluding couplet follows a quatrain. For example,
"Auf den Tod der unschuldigen Kinder":

> Israels zarte Frucht ward in den Nill versencket/
> Auf Pharaons Befehl/ als Moses ward gebohren.
> Doch Bethlems Kinder sind in eignem Blut erträncket/
> Als Gottes Kind erschin zu retten was verlohren.
> Wie wol! Weil Moses sie erlöst durchs rothe Meer!
> Und Jesus nur sein Blut gab vor die seinen her.
>
> (I, 85)

Like a sonnet this poem has a long exposition and a short conclusion. In longer epigrams Gryphius extends this form still further.
A twelve-line poem, "Über die Marter Catherine Königin von
Georgien," distinctly gives the impression of a defective sonnet but
is included in the epigrams:

> O schönstes Wunderwerck! O große Sinnen Macht!
> O höchste Königin der ie gekrönten Frawen!
> Geist welcher Zang und Brand kan anschawn sonder Grawen
> Der Abas höchste Gunst und schärffsten Grim verlacht!
> Gantz Persen steht bestürtzt und siht die Gaben an.
> Die diß Gemütt verwirfft. Gantz Persen steht und zaget
> In dem der lange Tod dich unverzagte plaget/
> Der zwar dein Fleisch/ nicht dich in Stücken reissen kan.
> So wird das schöne Gold durch heiße Glutt bewehrt.
> Ein Fürst kan andern wol/ nach dem er will/ gebieten:
> Du dir und der Natur/ du heissest dich kein wütten
> Empfinden/ welches dich die du es heist/ verzehrt.
>
> (I, 56)

There are many thematic resemblances between Gryphius's sonnets and epigrams, and it seems likely that he composed some of

---

Anthology in Italy to the Year 1800 and *The Greek Anthology in France.*
The argument that follows, regarding the relationship of Gryphius's epigrams
and his sonnets, is, in a sense, no more than an attempt to apply Hutton's
findings to German poetry.

them simultaneously, certainly in the same frame of mind. For example, the women's fashion of low-cut dresses, a favorite target of contemporary satirists, inspired both Gryphius's sonnet V, 71 and his epigram III, 32. The sonnet deals with a woman who is considered too old to expose her body; the epigram, with the incongruity of a girl's modestly hiding her face while baring her breasts. Epigram III, 55, "Grabschrifft eines vortrefflichen Redners," and sonnet III, 20, "Grabschrifft eins trefflichen Vorsprechers," are similarly related. Among the sonnets are a number of *Schmähgedichte,* poems of simple invective, that would have been more pungent as epigrams (for example, III, 30); while the epigram about Catherine von Georgien, a poem of extensive praise, would have been better in the finished form of a sonnet. Finally, there is a clear relationship between Gryphius's many religious sonnets and his religious epigrams. We may conclude that he saw the two forms as intimately related: that he considered them expressive in the same manner and for the same subject matter and that he thought it natural to turn from one to the other. The point is especially significant when one considers that Gryphius is without question the greatest German sonneteer of his age and perhaps of any age. A relationship recognized by so outstanding a practitioner of both the sonnet and the epigram is likely to be valid.

One cannot help but suspect that the negative evaluation of Gryphius's secular epigrams and the apparent refusal of some critics to investigate them more closely is a result of his treatment of sexual aberrations in some of his satiric epigrams. His tendency to see life from extreme points of view caused him to choose targets that are unsuitable for light barbs, while at the same time he retained the fashionable tone of ironic banter. The following examples illustrate both his shortcomings and his limited interest as a satirist:

    Auff den Levin
Man fragt warumb Levin zu freyen nicht gesonnen:
Er hat die Flavien, sein Kind, zu lib gewonnen.

                                       (II, 5)

    Auff eben denselben
Wofern man wie du sprichst Blutschänder soll vertreiben:
Wo wirst du/ und dein Kind/ und deine Schwester bleiben.

                                       (II, 6)

An Maeviam
Du klagst/ du seyst sehr schwach/ ich glaub es. Unser Knecht/
Hat in dem Stalle dich geschwächt ohn Red' und Recht.

(II, 17)

It must be conceded that these verses lack wit and permit a friction of manner and matter that constitutes a lapse of taste, probably even by Baroque standards. At the same time they are not uninteresting, for their faults are intimately connected with Gryphius's poetic virtues. They are a product of eccentric excess, an argumentative violence that far surpasses mere *argutia* and has in fact very little to do with the obligatory pointedness of the epigram.

Gryphius wrote a small group of poems that cannot be classed either as religious or as secular epigrams, although they have some of the qualities of both. These epigrams celebrating the speculative intellect of man and the scientific achievements of the seventeenth century include some of his best poems. They are unusual, and also highly significant, for they shed a flood of light on the seventeenth century's uneasy fusion of medieval and modern attitudes. The general philosophical problem has been discussed to some extent by Erich Trunz in a revealing article on Gryphius's sonnet "An die Sternen." [19] Trunz writes: "Seit Copernicus and Kepler sah der Gelehrte—und Gryphius gehörte zu den Gelehrten, er hielt damals in Leiden naturwissenschaftliche Vorlesungen—die Sterne in ihrer großen Ferne un Gesetzlichkeit. Das astronomische Weltbild, das sich in diesen Jahrzehnten rasch entwickelte, wurde religiös erlebt. Der Blick in die Sternenwelt jagte Gelehrten wie Laien Schauder über das Herz." [20] His essay is limited to one poem and to the subject of astronomy, but it can be applied to other poems and to the new attitude toward the intellect as such.

The religious poems we have discussed contain a certain amount of scientific imagery. Gryphius often expressed the miracle of the incarnation in terms of scientific impossibility. Thus Christ's birth

---

[19] Erich Trunz, "Andreas Gryphius' Gedicht 'An die Sternen,'" in *Interpretationen I: Deutsche Lyrik von Weckherlin bis Benn*, ed. Jost Schillemeit (Frankfort, 1965), pp. 19-28. See also Robert T. Clark, Jr., "Gryphius and the Night of Time," in *Wächter und Hüter, Festschrift für Hermann J. Weigand* (New Haven, Conn., 1957), pp. 56-66.

[20] Trunz, "Gryphius' Gedicht 'An die Sternen,'" p. 26.

is a reversal of astronomical law and God himself appears as a natural phenomenon, that is, light:

> Die ewig-lichte sonn erscheint zu mitternacht....
> Der himmel wird ein stall....
>
> (I, 20)

The same concept is applied to the crucifixion:

> Wen wundert, daß man nicht tag in dem mittag findet,
> Indem das wahre licht in todes-angst verschwindet?
>
> (I, 32)

Natural laws are reversed by a unique act of God. But they can also be transcended by man's ability to overcome his physical limitations through sheer force of mind. Gryphius expresses this dawning self-realization of the age of science in two complementary epigrams from book III (1663), numbers 22 and 23:

> Uber die Himmels Kugel
> Shaw hir des Himmels Bild/ diß hat ein Mensch erdacht/
> Der doch auff Erden saß: O übergroße Sinnen/
> Die mehr denn iemand schawt durch forschen nur gewinnen!
> Soll diß nicht himlisch seyn, was selber Himmel macht?
>
> Uber die Erd-Kugel
> Der Erden rundes Hauß das Vih und Menschen trägt/
> Ist noch nicht gantz beschawt/ doch ist es gantz gemessen.
> Was nie der Leib bezwang hat doch der Geist besessen.
> Der Land und Wellen Zill hir/ auch abwesend legt.   (Zill = Ziel)

On one level these verses return to the original function of the epigram, for both are invitations to contemplate a physical object. It is not surprising that the object is a globe. One needs only remember how often a globe is included among the paraphernalia of sixteenth- and seventeenth-century portraits, usually with the intention of underscoring the power of knowledge attributed to the subject, to realize that an aura of discovery and of mental as well as physical adventure must have been attached to these replicas of the world. The globe literally put the universe into man's hands. This is precisely how Gryphius uses it; the globe is a completely appropriate symbol for the mind's ability to control what the body

cannot: "Was nie der Leib bezwang hat doch der Geist besessen."
The mind owns what it knows or, as in these epigrams, what it
has measured. We have suddenly stepped beyond rhetoric and mannerism into a colder, clearer atmosphere to find the image of our
own age. Yet the characteristic theological language is still present:
"Soll diß nicht himlisch seyn, was selber Himmel macht?" That is,
man's rationality proves his divinity. One must realize that "Himmel machen" has nothing to do with an intuitive perception of God
but has a specifically rationalistic meaning, referring to globe making. Science did not yet inhibit faith but on the contrary still served it.

Several other epigrams deal similarly with human artifacts,
notably "An eine Bibliothec" (III, 21) and, most outstanding of all,
"Uber Nicolai Copernici Bild" (II, 2). We shall end our discussion
of Gryphius with an analysis of the latter poem, for there is hardly
another that both summarizes and transcends so many trends of
the Baroque epigram as well:

> Du dreymal weiser Geist/ du mehr denn großer Mann!
> Dem nicht die Nacht der Zeit die alles pochen kan/
> Dem nicht der herbe Neyd die Sinnen hat gebunden/
> Die Sinnen/ die den Lauff der Erden new gefunden.
> Der du der alten Träum und Dunckel widerlegt:
> Und Recht uns dargethan was lebt und was sich regt:
> Schaw itzund blüht dein Ruhm/ den als auff einem Wagen/
> Der Kreiß auff dem wir sind muß umb die Sonnen tragen.
> Wann diß was irrdisch ist/ wird mit der Zeit vergehn/
> Soll dein Lob unbewegt mit seiner Sonnen stehn.

The poem celebrates the discovery of the earth's revolution
around the sun. Its imagery of praise is based entirely on the discovery itself. Copernicus turns from the darkness and confusion of
ignorance—"Nacht der Zeit," "die alten Träum und Dunckel"—to
the sun, which is both the object of his discovery and the bright
symbol of knowledge. The mind fettered by irrational emotions,
"herbe Neyd," is contrasted in the next line with the motion of the
earth. This contrast results in the astonishing but satisfying association of planetary motion and the activity of the liberated mind. In
the exquisite imagery of the last four lines the earth carries Copernicus's fame as part of its newly discovered revolution around the
sun. The reference to "Wagen" recalls the chariot of the sun, symbol

of a mythology that has been discarded and replaced by the trium-
phant science of astronomy. Pagan mythology is succeeded by
Christian eschatology: at the end of time Copernicus's fame, now in
motion with the earth, will stand still, even as the sun will stand still
according to the Bible, even as the sun does stand still in time
according to Copernicus. This imagery owes a great deal to *galante
Lyrik*. Nothing is more common in Renaissance and Baroque
eulogies than sun imagery, culminating in *le roi soleil,* and other
natural phenomena were also used as flattering images. Gryphius
was pouring old wine into new bottles. Greeting the new age with
a voice trained in the schools of the past, he also succeeded in
affirming the old faith in his last two lines, where Copernicus is
raised into a Christian God's firmament like a hero of the ancients
to become a fixed star of the moderns.

Gryphius's significance as a Baroque epigrammatist is second
to none. Like Scheffler, he explored the outer confines of this limited
genre, and his rationality is as impassioned as Scheffler's mysticism,
in its studied clarity, is intellectual. Although Scheffler conveys a
sense of balance and Gryphius one of contrast and conflict, they
meet on a common ground where reason and intuition are bridged,
and thus they demonstrate together one of the functions of the
Baroque epigram. They both communicate flashes of lucid perception in the very process of describing the limitations of the conscious
mind.

CONCLUSION

ALTHOUGH THIS STUDY OF THE EPIGRAM HAS PROCEEDED mainly along thematic rather than historical lines, a certain chronological development can be outlined. The German epigram, a modern development of an older *Spruchform*, received its impetus from the Neo-Latin poets. It can be traced back to the sixteenth century in the verses of Ambrosius Lobwasser, apparently the first German writer to call a group of vernacular poems *Epigrammata*. Under the guidance of Opitz and the Neo-Latins the epigram developed very rapidly. What evolved was a complex, partly rhetorical, partly maneristic style that continued to have close ties with folk verse, which it often imitated and which was in turn influenced by it. This exchange is apparent in the relation of proverb and epigram as well as in the development of the literary inscription. Toward the middle of the seventeenth century the epigram became an ambitious form dealing not only with worldly subjects of all kinds but also with matters of life, death, and the afterlife. It employed linguistic and poetic devices that were highly subtle and original even when the themes and images themselves were derivative. Toward the end of the century the rationalistic, aphoristic trends of the epigram became dominant, as exemplified by the work of Wernicke; the complex poetic devices were gradually abandoned, and the epigram took its place as a minor form in an age of prose.

This historical outline opposes a widespread prejudice among the critics, many of whom see increasing decadence rather than increasing rationality in seventeenth-century German poetry. According to this prejudice the simplicity of an early style was corrupted by the complexity of a later style, and Baroque poetry became more hollow as the century advanced. This preconception is so axiomatic with certain critics that they ignore the facts if the facts do not fit their opinions. Here is a striking example: Rudolf Ibel, in order to denigrate Hofmannswaldau's *Grabschrifften*, compares a humorous epitaph on a fly to the poems of Czepko and Scheffler and laments the decline of the epigrammatic form: "So erscheint jetzt die Form eines Daniel von Czepko und Angelus Silesius, in der sich einst mystische Weisheit barg.... Übrig blieb die leere Form, die es möglichst wirkungsvoll und gewandt zu gebrauchen galt." [1] This statement clearly implies that Scheffler is the older poet and that *Der Cherubinische Wandersmann* considerably predates Hofmannswaldau's work. But the opposite is true: Hofmannswaldau was born in 1617, Scheffler in 1624; Hofmannswaldau's epitaphs were composed in the spring of 1643, [2] whereas *Der Cherubinische Wandersmann* was written some ten years later. Therefore, when Ibel claims that once ("einst") the two-line epigram had been great and mystical but that it later became trivial and decadent, he is simply constructing a chronology to suit his prejudice. The case is significant because it is typical, although the factual distortion is usually not as glaring.

This study contends that, on the contrary, Hofmannswaldau and Scheffler are not as unrelated in their poetic methods as one would think by dealing exclusively with their subject matter. We see a high point in the Baroque epigram where many literary historians see a low point, that is, at the heart of the rhetorical-manneristic movement; we have made an effort to show that even poets who are usually ruled out, such as Angelus Silesius, belong to that movement, whose basic feature appears to be an overriding concern with questions of language.

At the same time the epigram was a poem of emerging modern man, a supremely Western form. As such, it was more than a sounding board for language and poetic technique; it was also rational, pointed, didactic, and purposeful. This became more obvious as the seventeenth century advanced, but it had always been true to some extent: even the simple epigram tends to make a strong point. This

---

[1] Rudolf Ibel, *Hofman von Hofmannswaldau. Studien zur Erkenntnis deutscher Barockdichtung,* Germanische Studien, no. 59 (Berlin, 1928), p. 67.

[2] The evidence for this date is given by Karl Friebe, *Christian Hofman von Hofmannswaldaus Grabschriften* (Greifswald, 1893), pp. v, xix.

is best understood by comparing it with a small form that is not epigrammatic and comes from an entirely different tradition. I quote two Japanese haiku, chosen at random, the first anonymous, the second by Ki Tsurayuki: [3]

> Dimly in the dawn mist
> Of the Bay of Akashi
> Hidden by islands
> I dream of a boat.

> When I went to visit
> The girl I love so much,
> That winter night
> The river blew so cold
> That the plovers were crying.

Like epigrams these poems are short and specific in their evocation of scenery, but unlike epigrams they convey a mood and an atmosphere, not a rational point. In comparison with them almost any epigram quoted in this study appears didactic and almost obtrusively purposeful. When Gryphius ends one of his verses with the words "Mensch, nim dich selbst in acht!" he seems to speak for the hortatory nature of the genre as a whole. For no matter how playful the epigram becomes, no matter how recondite its themes, the poet's mind is sober, even if the verse itself is not. Even its mysticism is rational: the *Wandersmann* is "cherubic," not "seraphic"; in the language of the initiates this meant that the poems were a contribution to *Verstandesmystik,* not *Gefühlsmystik.*

In a social sense, too, the epigram was committed to the world on which it commented. Again, even its mysticism was shared, as in the Franckenberg circle where Czepko and Scheffler read their verses to like-minded friends. And as for worldly epigrams, they were used much as our parlor jokes are used today: they were strictly for company. Czepko made this point very succinctly in "An den Leser," one of his secular epigrams:

> Du darffst dir kein Pulpet zu diesem Buche machen,
> Noch in dem Zimmer es bedachtsam übersehn:

---

[3] Geoffrey Bownas and Anthony Thwaite, trans., *The Penguin Book of Japanese Verse* (Baltimore, Md., 1964), pp. 81, 83.

Denn ist es rechte Zeit, die Blätter umzudrehn,
Wenn du bey Tische sitzst und trinckst und pflegst zu lachen. [4]

Of course, a quest for conviviality and rationality does not always find a happy outcome. Questions of *ordo, ratio,* and the extent and nature of the objective world occupied the minds of poets as they occupied the minds of all thinking men of the seventeenth century. A new epistemology was also emerging, and the poets were quite aware that he who concentrates on an object long enough may find that it changes its aspect. Much of the fascination of the epigram lies in the fact that in its relentless pursuit of truth it sometimes turns out to be an inscription firmly engraved on a dreamlike thing.

After its Baroque triumphs the German epigram went into a long eclipse, although there have always been form-conscious poets who practiced it. Among them, apart from Schiller and Goethe at the height of their classical phase, were Mörike, Grillparzer, Stefan George, Karl Kraus and, perhaps most significantly, Bert Brecht. Paul Hankamer sees the seventeenth-century epigram as the forerunner of the romantic fragment. According to him, both forms are "der bezeichnende Ausdruck aphoristisch überspitzten Denkens, das in jeder Einzelung das Ganze begreifen will." [5] However, there is no evidence of systematic thought in any of the seventeenth-century epigrammatists, though some of them adopted bits and pieces of philosophical or theological systems. Nor did they have the consuming concern for a unified world view that characterized the early romantic poets, to which Hankamer refers. Friedrich Schlegel and Novalis made very large claims for the romantic fragment as a vital, indeed a basic form, but the epigrammatists, content to describe one piece of the world, have always been more modest. In fact, herein lies the epigram's limitation: a book of epigrams is often like an unstrung heap of beads. It offers flashes of perception, as much as the eye or the mind can focus on at one time, but it does not provide a connection between one thing and another, between one moment and the next. Lessing was aware of this limitation when he wrote "Die Sinngedichte über sich selbst":

[4] Czepko, *Weltliche Dichtungen,* p. 361.
[5] Hankamer, *Die Sprache,* p. 173.

Weiß uns der Leser auch für unsre Kürze Dank?
Wohl kaum. Denn Kürze wird durch Vielheit leider lang. [6]

Recently, however, the epigram seems to be gaining ground again. There is abundant evidence that contemporary poets are impatient with subjective lyricism, inspired states of mind, and the expression of personal emotions. This has led some of them back to the cool, terse craft of the epigram. Brecht, who not only wrote epigrams but also had some theoretic interest in them, seems to be the patron saint of this incipient revival. [7] A glance at two of his epigrammatic verses may therefore be a fit conclusion:

> Der Rauch
> Das kleine Haus unter Bäumen am See
> Vom Dach steigt Rauch.
> Fehlte er
> Wie trostlos dann wären
> Haus Bäume und See.

> Die Maske des Bösen
> An meiner Wand hängt ein japanisches Holzwerk
> Maske eines bösen Dämons, bemalt mit Goldlack.
> Mitfühlend sehe ich
> Die geschwollenen Stirnader, andeutend
> Wie anstrengend es ist, böse zu sein. [8]

Superficially the first of these seems to be influenced by the haiku, but on second sight it becomes apparent that the poem is a perfect bipartite epigram of which Lessing would have approved. The first two lines give the object, the exposition; the last three, the thought, the resolution. The resolution gravely defines man's relation to nature: only the cultivated scene and the human landscape convey comfort. The second poem is witty, pithy, also bipartite, and in the nature of an inscription. It describes evil as a tangible, man-made household object, detailed and visible, "bemalt mit Goldlack." The verse pertains to a single object and yet is addressed to humanity

---

[6] Lessing, *Werke,* I: 34.

[7] See Bertolt Brecht, *Über Lyrik,* Edition Suhrkamp (Frankfort, 1964), pp. 89-93.

[8] Bertolt Brecht, *Gedichte und Lieder* (Frankfort, 1962), pp. 151, 153.

at large with its muted, optimistic point that it is easier to be good than evil.

It seems fairly obvious that both these poems, while employing a highly modern idiom, belong to the epigrammatic tradition with which we have dealt. If recent German poets have indeed followed Brecht's example and the epigram is entering into a phase of renewed vigor, this study of the Baroque epigram may have a modest relevance from a modern perspective. Certainly the epigram as a genre should be able to withstand almost any change of times and conditions, for as Scaliger wrote several hundred years ago, there are as many kinds of epigrams as there are kinds of things:

Epigrammatum autem genera tot sunt, quot rerum.

WORKS CITED

(Note: References to clearly extraneous works, such as poems by Shakespeare, Goethe, and Brecht, have been omitted.)

AGRICOLA, JOHANN. "Siebenhundert vnd Fünfftzig Deutsche Sprichwörter, ernewert vnd gebessert durch Johan. Agricola. Gedruckt nach der Geburt Christi im Jar M.D. CLVII." In *Volksbücher des 16. Jahrhunderts,* edited by Felix Bobertag, pp. 411-32. Deutsche National Literatur, vol 25. Berlin, n.d.

ALTHAUS, HORST. *Johann Schefflers "Cherubinischer Wandersmann": Mystik und Dichtung.* Beiträge zur deutschen Philologie, vol. 9. Giessen, 1956.

ARENS, FRITZ WIKTOR, ed. *Die Inschriften der Stadt Mainz von frühmittelalterlicher Zeit bis 1650.* Die deutschen Inschriften, vol. 2. Stuttgart, 1948.

BEUTLER, ERNST. *Vom griechischen Epigramm im 18. Jahrhundert.* Probefahrten, vol. 15. Leipzig 1909. (Partially reprinted in *Das Epigramm. Zur Geschichte einer inschriftlichen und literarischen Gattung,* edited by Gerhard Pfohl, pp. 352-416. Wege der Forschung. Darmstadt, 1969.)

BÖCKMANN, PAUL. *Formgeschichte der deutschen Dichtung.* Vol. 1. Hamburg, 1965.

BRECHT, FRANZ JOSEF. "Motiv- und Typengeschichte des griechischen Spottepigramms." *Philologus,* suppl. vol 22, part 2 (1930), pp. 1-114 passim.

BROWN, NORMAN O. *Life against Death: The Psychoanalytical Meaning of History.* Middletown, Conn., 1959.

CLARK, ROBERT T., JR. "Gryphius and the Night of Time." In *Wächter und Hüter, Festschrift für Hermann J. Weigand,* pp. 56-66. New Haven, Conn., 1957.

CONRADY, KARL OTTO. *Lateinische Dichtungstradition und deutsche Lyrik des 17. Jahrhunderts.* Bonn, 1962.

CURTIUS, ERNST ROBERT. *Europäische Literatur und lateinisches Mittelalter.* Berne, 1948.

CYSARZ, HERBERT. *Deutsche Barockdichtung.* Leipzig, 1924.

———. *Deutscher Barock in der Lyrik.* Leipzig, 1936.

CZEPKO, DANIEL VON. *Geistliche Dichtungen.* Edited by Werner Milch. Breslau, 1932.

———. *Weltliche Dichtungen.* Edited by Werner Milch. Breslau, 1932.

DENKER, HEINRICH. *Ein Beitrag zur litterarischen Würdigung Friedrichs von Logau.* Dissertation, University of Göttingen, 1889.

DRAHEIM, HANS. *Deutsche Reime. Inschriften des 15. Jahrhunderts und der folgenden.* Berlin, 1883.

DRESELLY, ANTON. *Grabschriften, Marterl-, Bildstöckl- und Totenbrett-Verse, dann Hausinschriften, Wohn- und Trinkstuben-Reime, Geräthe-Inschriften und andere.* Salzburg, 1900.

ELLINGER, GEORG. *Angelus Silesius. Ein Lebensbild.* Breslau, 1927.

ERB, THERESE. *Die Pointe in der Dichtung von Barock und Aufklärung.* Bonn, 1929.

FORCK, L. *Deutsche Inschriften an Haus und Geräth.* Berlin, 1865.

FRICKE, GERHARD. *Die Bildlichkeit in der Dichtung des Andreas Gryphius.* Berlin, 1933.

FRIEBE, KARL. *Christian Hofman von Hofmannswaldaus Grabschriften.* Greifswald, 1893.

GERVINUS, GEORG GOTTFRIED. *Handbuch der Geschichte der poetischen National-Literatur der Deutschen.* Leipzig, 1842.

GOEDEKE, KARL. *Grundriss zur Geschichte der deutschen Dichtung.* 2d ed. Dresden, 1886.

GRIMMELSHAUSEN, JOHANN JAKOB CHRISTOPH VON. *Simplicianische Schriften.* Edited by Alfred Kelletat. Darmstadt, 1965.

GROB, JOHANN. Epigramme. Edited by Axel Lindqvist. Bibliothek des literarischen Vereins in Stuttgart, vol. 273. Leipzig, 1929.

GRYPHIUS, ANDREAS. *Gesamtausgabe der deutschprachigen Werke.* Vol. 1, *Sonette,* edited by Hugh Powell, Tubingen, 1963; vol. 2, *Oden und Epigramme,* edited by Marian Szyrocki, Tubingen, 1964. Neudrucke deutscher Literaturwerke, new ser., vols. 9 and 10.

HANKAMER, PAUL. *Die Sprache. Ihr Begriff und ihre Deutung im sechzehnten und siebzehnten Jahrhundert.* Bonn, 1927.

HECKEL, HANS. *Geschichte der deutschen Literatur in Schlesien.* Vol 1. Breslau, 1929.

HEMPEL, PAUL. *Die Kunst Friedrichs von Logau.* Palaestra, vol. 130. Berlin, 1917.

HERDER, JOHANN GOTTFRIED. "Anmerkungen über das griechische Epigramm." In *Herders Sämmtliche Werke,* edited by Bernhard Suphan, 15: 337-92. Berlin, 1888.

HEUSCHKEL, WALTER. *Untersuchungen über Ramlers und Lessings Bearbeitung von Sinngedichten Logaus.* Dissertation, University of Jena, 1901.

HOFMANNSWALDAU, HOFMANN VON. *Geistliche Oden, vermischte Gedichte und poetische Grabschrifften.* Breslau, 1696.

HÖPFNER, ERNST. *Reformbestrebungen auf dem Gebiete der deutschen Dichtung des XVI. und XVII. Jahrhunderts.* Jahresbericht des K. Wilhelm-Gymnasium in Berlin. Berlin, 1866.

HUDSON, HOYT HOPEWELL. *The Epigram in the English Renaissance.* Princeton, N. J., 1947.

HUTTON, JAMES, *The Greek Anthology in France.* Cornell Studies in Classical Philology, vol. 28. Ithaca, N. Y., 1946.

――――. *The Greek Anthology in Italy to the Year 1800.* Cornell Studies in English, vol. 23. Ithaca, N. Y., 1935.

IBEL, RUDOLF. *Hofman von Hofmannswaldau. Studien zur Erkenntnis deutscher Barockdichtung.* Germanische Studien, no. 59. Berlin, 1928.

JOLLES, ANDRÉ. *Einfache Formen.* Halle, 1956.

JÖNS, DIETRICH WALTER. *Das "Sinnen-Bild." Studien zur allegorischen Bildlichkeit bei Andreas Gryphius.* Stuttgart, 1966.

KAYSER, WOLFGANG. "Böhmes Natursprachenlehre und ihre Grundlagen." *Euphorion* 31 (1930): 521-62.

KEIL, ROBERT, and KEIL, RICHARD. *Die deutschen Stammbücher des sechzehnten bis neunzehnten Jahrhunderts.* Berlin, 1893.

LESSING, GOTTHOLD EPHRAIM. "Zerstreute Anmerkungen über das Epigramm und einige der vornehmsten Epigrammatisten." In *Lessings Werke,* edited by Julius Petersen and Waldemar von Olshausen, 14: 118-208. Leipzig, n.d.

LEVY, RICHARD. *Martial und die deutsche Epigrammatik des siebzehnten Jahrhunderts.* Stuttgart, 1903.

LINDQVIST, AXEL. *Det tyske 1600-Tals-epigrammets motiv och tendenser.* Göteborg Högskolas årsskrift, vol. 55. Göteborg, 1949. (Translated into German in *Das Epigramm. Zur Geschichte einer inschriftlichen und literarischen Gattung,* edited by Gerhard Pfohl, pp. 287-352. Darmstadt, 1969.)

LOBWASSER, AMBROSIUS. *Deutsche Zierliche Epigrammata von allen Ständen vnd leuten in gemein.* N.p., 1634.

LOGAU, FRIEDRICH VON. *Friedrichs von Logau sämmtliche Sinngedichte.* Edited by Gustav Eitner. Bibliothek des Litterarischen Vereins in Stuttgart, vol. 113. Tubingen, 1872.

LUNDING, ERIK. "Stand und Aufgaben der deutschen Barockforschung." *Orbis Litterarum* 8 (1950): 27-91.

LUTHER, MARTIN. *Luthers Sprichwörtersammlung.* Edited by Ernst Otto Thiele. Weimar, 1900.

MARKWARDT, BRUNO. *Geschichte der deutschen Poetik.* Vol. 1. Berlin, 1937.

MAROT, CLÉMENT. *Œuvres Complètes.* Vol. 2. Paris, 1824.

MERKER, PAUL, and STAMMLER, WOLFGANG. *Reallexikon der deutschen Literaturgeschichte.* 2d ed. Berlin, 1964.

MÖLL, OTTO E. *Sprichwörter-Bibliographie.* Frankfort, 1958.

MÖNCH, WALTER. *Das Sonnet. Gestalt und Geschichte.* Heidelberg, 1955.

MORE, SIR THOMAS. *The Latin Epigrams of Thomas More.* Edited with translations and notes by Leicester Bradner and Charles Arthur Lynch. Chicago, 1953.

MORHOF, DANIEL GEORG. *Unterricht von der teutschen Sprache und Poesie.* 3d ed. Leipzig, 1718.

MÜLLER, GÜNTHER. *Geschichte des deutschen Liedes.* Munich, 1925.

NEUKIRCH, BENJAMIN. *Benjamin Neukirchs Anthologie... erster theil.* Edited by Angelo George de Capua and Ernst Alfred Philippson. Neudrucke deutscher Literaturwerke, new ser., vol. 1. Tubingen, 1961.

NEUMANN, GERHARD, ed. *Deutsche Epigramme.* Stuttgart, 1969.

OPITZ, MARTIN. *Ausgewählte Dichtungen von Martin Opitz.* Edited by Julius Tittmann. Deutsche Dichter des siebzehnten Jahrhunderts, vol. 1. Leipzig, 1869.

———. *Buch von der deutschen Poeterey (1624).* Edited by Wilhelm Braune and Richard Alewyn. Neudrucke deutscher Literaturwerke, new ser., vol. 8. Tubingen, 1963.

———. *Teutsche Poemata.* Edited by Georg Witkowski. Neudrucke deutscher Litteraturwerke, nos. 189-92. Halle, 1902.

PEEK, WERNER, *Griechische Grabgedichte. Griechisch und deutsch.* Schriften und Quellen der alten Welt, vol. 7. Berlin, 1960.

PETSCH, ROBERT. *Spruchdichtung des Volkes.* Halle, 1938.

PFOHL, GERHARD, ed. *Das Epigramm. Zur Geschichte einer inschriftlichen und literarischen Gattung.* Darmstadt, 1969.

PISSIN, RAYMOND. "Friedrich von Logau und die Gegenwart." *Berliner Hefte* 1 (1946): 539-43.

PREISENDANZ, WOLFGANG. *Die Spruchform in der Lyrik des alten Goethe und ihre Vorgeschichte seit Opitz.* Heidelberg, 1952.

RIMBACH, GÜNTHER C. "Das Epigramm und die Barockpoetik." *Jahrbuch der deutschen Schillergesellschaft* 14 (1970): 100-31.

RUBENSOHN, MAX. *Griechische Epigramme und andere kleinere Dichtungen in deutschen Übersetzungen des XVI. und XVII. Jahrhunderts.* Bibliothek älterer deutscher Übersetzungen, vols. 2-5. Weimar, 1897.

SACHS, HANS. *Hans Sachs.* Edited by Adelbert von Keller and Edmund Heinrich Goetze. Bibliothek des Litterarischen Vereins in Stuttgart, vol. 207. Tubingen, 1895.

SAMMONS, JEFFREY L. *Angelus Silesius.* New York, 1967.

SCHEFFLER, JOHANN. *Angelus Silesius. Sämtliche Poetische Werke in drei Bänden.* Edited by Hans Ludwig Held. Munich, 1949.

SCHLEGEL, FRIEDRICH. *Anfangspunkte des christlichen Nachdenkens nach den Sprüchen des cherubinischen Wandersmanns (1820).* Edited by Hans Ludwig Held. Munich, 1917.

SCHÖNE, ALBRECHT. *Emblematik und Drama im Zeitalter des Barock.* Munich, 1964.

SCHUBERT, ERNST, ed. *Die Inschriften der Stadt Naumburg an der Saale.* Die deutschen Inschriften, vol. 7. Stuttgart, 1960.

SEEL, OTTO. "Ansatz zu einer Martial-Interpretation." In *Das Epigramm. Zur Geschichte einer inschriftlichen und literarischen Gattung,* edited by Gerhard Pfohl, pp. 153-87. Darmstadt, 1969.

SEILER, FRIEDRICH. *Sprichwörterkunde.* Munich, 1922.

SEYPPEL, JOACHIM H. "Freedom and the mystical union in *Der Cherubinische Wandersmann.*" *Germanic Review* 32 (1957): 93-112.

SPAHR, BLAKE LEE. "Dogs and Doggerel in the German Baroque." *Journal of English and Germanic Philology* 54 (1955): 380-86.

SPÖRRI, ELISABETH. *Der Cherubinische Wandersmann als Kuntswerk.* Zürcher Beiträge zur deutschen Sprach- und Stilgeschichte, no. 2. Zurich, 1947.

SZYROCKI, MARIAN. *Andreas Gryphius, sein Leben und Werk.* Tubingen, 1964.

TAYLOR, HENRY OSBORN. *Erasmus and Luther.* New York, 1962.

TRUNZ, ERICH. "Andreas Gryphius' Gedicht 'An die Sternen.'" In *Interpretationen I: Deutsche Lyrik von Weckherlin bis Benn,* edited by Jost Schillemeit, pp. 19-28. Frankfort, 1965.

――――. "Die deutschen Übersetzungen des Hugenottenpsalters." *Euphorion* 29 (1928): 578-617.

――――. "Die Entwicklung des barocken Langverses." *Euphorion* 39 (1938): 427-69.

URBAN, ERICH. *Owenus und die deutschen Epigrammatiker des XVII. Jahrhunderts.* Litterarhistorische Forschungen, vol. 11. Berlin, 1900.

VIËTOR, KARL. *Geist und Form.* Bonn, 1952.

WALDBERG, MAX VON. *Die deutsche Renaissance-Lyrik.* Berlin, 1888.

WALDBERG, MAX VON. *Die galante Lyrik.* Quellen und Forschungen zur Spach- und Culturgeschichte der Deutschen, vol. 56. Strasburg, 1885.

WATTENBACH, WILHELM. *Das Schriftwesen im Mittelalter.* Leipzig, 1896.

WERNICKE, CHRISTIAN. *Christian Wernicke's Epigramme.* Edited by Rudolf Pechel. Palaestra, vol. 81. Berlin, 1909.

WIESE, BENNO VON. "Die Antithetik in den Alexandrinern des Angelus Silesius." *Euphorion* 29 (1928): 503-22. (Reprinted in *Deutsche Barockforschung,* edited by Richard Alewyn, pp. 260-84. Cologne, 1966.)

ZINCGREF, JULIUS WILHELM. *Auserlesene Gedichte deutscher Poeten, gesammelt von Julius Wilhelm Zinkgref, 1624.* Edited by Wilhelm Braune. Neudrucke deutscher Litteraturwerke, vol. 15. Halle, 1879.

INDEX